MATCH FISHING
A GUIDE TO COMPETITIVE ANGLING

First published in Great Britain in 1993
by Boxtree Limited

Text and Photographs © EMAP Pursuit Publishing Ltd 1993

1 3 5 7 9 10 8 6 4 2

Edited by Helen Douglas Cooper
Designed by Anita Ruddell

Colour origination in Hong Kong by Rainbow Graphics
Printed and bound in Great Britain by Bath Press Colour Books

Boxtree Limited
Broadwall House
21 Broadwall
London SE1 9PL

A CIP catalogue entry for this book is available from the British Library.

ISBN 1 85283 443 9

MATCH FISHING
A GUIDE TO COMPETITIVE ANGLING

Edited by Kevin Wilmot
with a foreword by Dave Roper

BⓈXTREE

**Former world
champion Dave Roper
with bonus canal
bream.**

CONTENTS

ACKNOWLEDGEMENTS

The editor and publishers would
like to thank the following:

Macolm Lane for use of his illustrations.

Bob Atkins and Angus Murray
for use of their photographs.

Thanks to all of the anglers who
have helped contribute to
Improve Your Coarse Fishing magazine
since its launch in 1991.

FOREWORD

I suppose my match fishing career started when I was about eight years old, when three of us used to visit a farm pond suitably geared up with garden canes, string and bent pins. We caught rudd on a 'first to 10' basis. Big ones of over 3 oz counted as two. Believe me it was easier winning the World Championships! Things have, of course, changed since then. Match anglers have been responsible for the creation of a multi-million pound industry of which I am proud, in a small way, to have been a part. Whether or not I could have been an achiever in some other sport or occupation, I will never know. What I do know is that, given my time again, I would not change a thing. What started out as an innocent casual hobby grew into an absolute obsession that was carried out at the expense of everything else.

Some of the characters I have met, and some of the experiences I have enjoyed are worth sharing, such as the time in 1961 when Ted Carter opened up his tackle shop in Church Street, Preston. It was to become not only the largest in the immediate area, but one of the first angling mega-stores in England. Then it was only a small shop. Ted was famous not only as a brilliant angler, but also for producing the Ted Carter Match Special, a wonderful 11 ft, Spanish-reed canal rod. I remember paying £6.17s.6d for one – and I was on my way.

The two greatest influences on my match fishing career were without doubt Ivan Marks and Kevin Ashurst. Their contributions over the years were priceless. When I first started fishing the Irish festivals during the early 1970s, Ivan was usually present. He used to take Dave Brogden and me fishing on free days and we learned an enormous amount. On one day on the River Suck, Ivan took half a dozen of my prized, home-made peacock wagglers and made one great big float out of them. He then fished a fixed float 15 feet deep along the middle. I wonder how many of today's matchmen would show such initiative.

Kevin was different. To be honest he frightened me a little. He could achieve more with one look than anybody else I know. On one occasion I was fishing a match at Foulridge Reservoir in Lancashire and I drew on the next peg to Kevin. The whistle went and we all started to feed a long-distance legering swim. I pulled back my catapult elastic with an oversized ball of groundbait and one strand of the elastic snapped. The ball of groundbait shot up into the air and landed right in front of Kevin, 10 yd out into the lake. I can still remember the look on Kevin's face. Since then, of course, I have travelled all over Europe with Kevin and other equally talented match anglers, and to them all I owe a tremendous debt.

Match fishing is a great sport and if you have chosen to

concentrate on it in preference to other aspects of angling, I know you won't be disappointed. The one thing that was missing during my early match fishing career was a book such as this one. We had to rely very much on trial and error. Of course, first-hand experience is vital when you are attempting to achieve any degree of success in the sport, but as you are about to discover for yourselves, a good book can be a tremendous help as well.

Dave Roper

The all-important draw can make or break a match-man's day.

THE APPEAL OF MATCH FISHING

When someone takes up angling for the first time, the main priority is to catch fish. What sort of fish is largely immaterial. As long as the float goes under, they're happy. However, as the angler becomes more proficient, there usually comes a time when he wants to specialise. It might stem from a chance conversation in a fishing tackle shop, a story or a feature he has read in the angling press, or just an inner feeling that one branch of fishing is more interesting, enjoyable or exciting than any other.

For some, the excitement comes in the pursuit of a big fish. The term 'specimen hunter' springs to mind, although most would now prefer to be called 'specialist anglers'. Many such anglers think little of spending a whole season trying to catch a single, known fish – carp, barbel or whatever. Others - and these can equally be called specialists – enjoy pitting their wits against their fellow fishermen as well as against the fish, and it is these who are known as match anglers.

Perhaps their interest has stirred during a trip with friends to the local canal, when as the day progressed it gradually became apparent that there was a sense of competition in the air. The jocular banter was replaced by tense silence as each one tried to catch more than this friends, now his rivals as well. More likely they joined a local club that held matches on a favourite venue, where the angler could pit his wits against others. These club contests are where most of the top match anglers started their 'careers'.

Even impromptu affairs can be regarded as matches, and

many anglers, once they have fished a match or two, are hooked for life. Not for them the solitary existence of the specimen hunter or the relaxed deck-chair stints of the out-and-out pleasure anglers. Once the competitive bug has hit, there's no getting away from it.

But perhaps we are running before we can walk. Let's first of all ask one vitally important question. What is match fishing? To an angler who has been fishing matches for years, that might seem a ridiculous question, but what about the one who is still getting to grips with the sport? How could he know what is involved in a fishing match?

It's quite simple really. A fishing match involves a row of anglers placed equal distances apart – usually a little more than 15 m – with each trying to catch a greater weight of fish than the rest during a set time, usually between two and six hours.

The competitors meet at an allotted time and place beforehand, where they pay an entrance fee and sometimes optional pools before making the draw for 'pegs' out of a hat. Ideally, there are the same number of pegs in the hat as there are competitors in the match. Once the angler has drawn his peg, he makes his way along the waterside with his tackle until he reaches the swim tagged with the number he has drawn. This is where he has to fish for the whole of the contest.

Some of the more popular match venues are permanently pegged, meaning that there are permanent markers – concrete posts, for example – placed at equal distances along the bank, to save the match organiser having to peg the stretch before every contest. Once the angler has reached his swim – in match fishing the swim is usually known as the 'peg' – he tackles up and awaits a signal telling him to start to fish. On no account must he fish before the signal, although he can usually mix groundbait, position his keepnet and test the depth of the water in front him with a float and plummet. Plumbing the depth with a swimfeeder is not allowed as it opens the door to cheating if anyone is that way inclined.

At the end of the contest a whistle is blown by the organiser or somebody mandated by him to tell everyone to stop fishing immediately. Stewards then walk along the bank weighing each angler's catch, which they have stored in a keepnet. Special anglers' scales are used, which are often accurate to within ¼ oz. Once all the anglers have been weighed in, the results are calculated and prizes presented to those who have taken the biggest catches.

In general terms, that is how a match works, and from that you might assume that match fishing is a pretty serious business. Of course it is, but ask any match angler why he has chosen this branch of the sport to pursue, and he will answer:

because he enjoys it.

From the smallest Sunday morning club contest to the largest 'open' event, there's always a buzz of excitement during the draw as each angler tries to pick out the winning peg. Then there's the anticipation as they wait, tackle at the ready, for the match to start, the enjoyment of catching fish, and the satisfaction of knowing they have beaten their rivals. And usually the winner can feel highly satisfied. After all, match fishing by its very nature puts constraints upon those who pursue it. Who apart from a match angler would choose to be told where he has to fish, at the most difficult time of the day for fishing, and only 20 paces away from two other anglers?

Of course, there's also the disappointment of choosing the wrong method to fish and knowing you have done so after the event; the frustration of losing that all-important fish at the net; the annoyance of finishing just out of the prize money . . . but that all just makes most match anglers want to go out and do better next time.

A match can take many forms. At its most basic level, it's simply a group of friends fishing in a line to see who catches the most – something to add a little spice to a day's pleasure fishing. Then there are club events, where members of a club meet up and fish a match together. At the end of the season, someone is usually crowned club champion. On the next rung of the ladder are the open events, contests that are available to any angler in the country to fish as long as he buys a ticket in advance.

Team matches are another question altogether. Here, teams of up to 12 anglers compete against each other with the results being decided on a points basis. One member of each team is placed in each section and the anglers are awarded points according to where they finish in that section. The pinnacle of team events are the National Championships, now fishable by many more than just match angling's elite, thanks to the divisional system. At present there are six National Federation of Anglers divisions, each comprising 90 teams of 12 anglers. A lot of people go match fishing!

However seriously you take it, match fishing is ultimately just another branch of angling to be enjoyed, just like specimen hunting and pleasure fishing. Winning is a bonus – but it's great!

11

CHAPTER ONE

HOW TO START

Above: You're never too young to start match fishing.

Opposite: Some anglers learn their match fishing skills on rivers.

So you want to take up match fishing? Welcome to the ranks of thousands of anglers who fish matches every week or every month of the season. For some, three matches a week is not enough. These are the open match anglers, willing to spend a great deal of money in pursuit of glory and prize winnings. They think nothing of travelling the length and breadth of the country in pursuit of good contests, and nothing less than total commitment is enough for them.

12

Others prefer one weekend match, still possibly an open event and to be taken just as seriously, while for many a Sunday morning trip with their local club is the highlight of the week. The beginner to match fishing would do best to start with these club contests, but even this branch of match fishing is not to be taken lightly. Even the smallest, most friendly of contests usually has cash winnings at stake, and wouldn't you rather be walking up to receive the money afterwards than standing clapping the winner?

Many anglers make the mistake of thinking they can run before they have learned to walk. They decide that they know a certain venue like the back of their hands and can take on the world. So they fish an open match against some of the best in the business and are beaten out of sight. They try again. The same thing happens. This is the quickest way to destroy a would-be match angler. You might know a lot about a certain venue, but there's a world of difference between choosing your swim and having it chosen for you. That's the whole essence of match fishing. You can't choose your spot. This has happened to many match fishing beginners, especially youngsters, who decide to fish open matches without graduating through the club ranks first. Most of today's top matchmen served a club apprenticeship. Follow their lead and one day you too could be fishing for your country.

There are several ways of joining a club. Many tackle shops sell membership books for various clubs in their area, especially if they control some fishing of their own. Then there are those clubs that are formed through a pub. These are very common and often offer the best chance of making friends with the other club members. Enjoying a drink after the match is a good time to talk tactics, listening to others about how they fished the match, trying to assess where you went wrong, and even offering advice of your own. As you become increasingly successful, you will find that more and more club members are wanting to buy you drinks and pick your brain! Other clubs are formed purely and simply to hold matches and a call to the secretary will usually bring you membership. Again your local tackle shop can help here. Some limited-member clubs have waiting lists to which you can add your name until being asked to join officially. These are often clubs with good fisheries that hold most if not all of their matches on their own water.

You should think carefully before deciding to join one particular club. Is it right for you? Are some of your friends already members? Does it hold enough matches for you, or too many? Are the matches fished at the most convenient time? Are you familiar with the venues? How good are the other anglers who fish the club matches? The question of venues is a very important one. Many of the country's top match anglers started by joining a club that fished its matches on familiar venues on which they felt proficient.

As an example, an angler might believe, with good reason, that he has mastered his local river. He catches consistently more than others fishing on the same stretch. What better way to test his ability than by joining a local club that holds matches there, because there's only one way to discover just how proficient he is – by fishing a match against others on the same venue. There's nothing like a match for bringing an angler down a peg or two, but it can also be a tremendous boost to confidence. It might destroy a budding match angler completely if he was to pick a club that holds many of its matches on a local lake if he has done most of his fishing on the river. Of course, some might want to do this, on the assumption that the best way to learn is to fish against others and probably take a good hiding into the bargain. However, you need a thick skin to do this more than a few times!

Another way in which many anglers approach match fishing is to make their decision. Then before spending valuable time and money fishing matches – and being beaten – they do plenty of watching, perhaps sacrificing a few Sundays to sit behind their favourite anglers and see how they tackle a particular venue. Most matchmen will be delighted to chat about baits and methods . . . after the contest has finished. During the event, it would be far better to keep your distance. Check with the competitor that he doesn't mind you sitting behind him, stay well back, where he suggests you settle, and watch and learn. Don't speak unless you are spoken to. Match anglers are many and varied. Some find that a keen spectator, asking the right sort of questions, is an aid to their concentration. These are the ones who are only too keen to talk to you before, during and after the match. However, others take the opposite view and look upon spectators as unnecessary distractions. You'll soon discover which camp your matchman lies in.

The question of finances is obviously an important one. At the draw for most matches, you'll pay your entry fee and probably have the chance to enter the optional pools. You don't have to enter them, but if you don't and you win the match, you don't win anything from the pools. 'Your' money goes to the runner-up, or the highest-placed angler who entered the pools. However, many club matches are well within the reach of most anglers' pockets and £3 will usually see you 'all the way' in the pools. Even if finances dictate that you cannot afford to enter all the pools, many club and open matches divide up their pools system, allowing you to be selective as to which pools you want to enter. It's worth checking whether your chosen club allows this before you

15

Could you handle a 'gallery' like this?

decide to join. For example, you might want to enter the section pool only. This means that you are entering the pool against the others in your section of, say, 10 anglers. Separate pools are run taking in the whole of the match. Don't put too much pressure on yourself by having a full bet. Build up your confidence with a few good section wins and you'll soon be ready to go 'all the way'.

Club matches take several forms. Most will be simple individual events where the angler who catches the biggest weight of fish is the winner. However, there are other types of contest that add a little excitement to the proceedings, such as pairs events where two anglers pair up – either by choice or, more often, by being drawn out of the hat – and fish against other pairs, the pair with the highest aggregate weight being declared the winners. Then there are inter-club events where one club takes on another. These are usually enjoyable days out, with one club travelling to a venue of the other club's choice before returning the favour later on in the season. These events are very popular and some inter-club challenges have been taking place twice a season for many years. It's certainly a way to make new friends and fish new and exciting venues. Handicap matches used to be more popular than they are now. These are events where the match

16

The weigh-in.

organiser assesses each competitor and issues them with a handicap according to their ability. For example, a beginner might be given a 100 per cent start, in other words his catch is doubled, whereas an expert might have to fish without the benefit of any help at all.

When you enter your first match, there are a few golden rules to follow. First, arrive at the headquarters early. It might be a pub, or it might be at the venue. If it's at the venue, take a little time to go and have a look at the water. Already you will be forming ideas on how you are going to fish. If the headquarters is a pub, have a cup of tea. Decide whether you want anything to eat before the draw. Most pub headquarters now lay on food, and you might be too busy to eat anything

17

once the match has started. When it comes to the draw, draw early. Don't listen to those anglers who insist on telling you that it's best to draw late. An early draw gives you the best possible chance of a good peg. A late draw obviously means that more of the good pegs will have been taken. Of course, so will more of the bad ones, but you're not interested in those are you? Think positive! After the draw, try to discover as much about your peg as you can by asking friends and local experts, some of whom will be only too pleased to show off their knowledge. Take it all in, but remember that the best anglers are those who listen and then use their own skills and experience to build on what they have been told. Copy an expert and you can only ever be as good as him. Innovate and you'll be better.

Once you have found your peg, place your tackle down beside you gently and take a little time to assess the water. Ask yourself several questions. Have you ever fished your swim, or a neighbouring one, before? If so, what have you learned about it? Even if you haven't fished it, there is a lot to be learned just by looking. Are there any good features like overhanging trees, or places on a river where the flow seems to have picked up. Plumb the depth. Are there any shelves or ledges where the depth suddenly drops off? This can act as a magnet to fish. Places such as these are all potential fish-holding areas so make a mental note of them before the match starts. Even if they produce one or two 'bonus' fish, they were worth fishing, weren't they?

It's all too easy to fish a match in your own little world, totally oblivious to what's going on around you. This is a mistake. If the angler at the next peg suddenly starts catching bream on the swimfeeder while you're polefishing for small fish, you need to know about it. Match fishing success is almost as much about reacting to different situations as it is about angling ability. You'll need to know what your neighbour's up to, especially if he is one of the club experts. Of course, don't spend so much time looking at the anglers either side that you don't concentrate on your job – catching fish. Some matchmen look as if they are tennis-match spectators and end up frustrated also-rans. The ideal situation is when the anglers on either side spend all day watching you – and you're too busy catching fish to notice them!

Once the match is finished, stop fishing immediately, pack your tackle away, taking care to remove any litter, and await the scales. Now here's another important point. When your catch is weighed, watch carefully. Every ounce now is vital. Make sure the scales are 'zeroed' before each angler's catch is weighed. All sets of scales have a small setting wheel at the back that is turned to move the needle to the zero position. As the weight sling becomes wet and slimy with each weighing, it weighs a little more and could give the next angler some advantage unless the scales are zeroed every time. Check the weight as well. If you feel you're being 'done', speak out. It's no use moaning afterwards that you just missed out on a prize and you should have been given ½ oz extra. Finally, make certain that your weight has been correctly recorded on the weigh board, especially that your pounds have been put in the pounds column and your ounces in the ounces column. Fractions of ounces are usually recorded either as fractions or as drams. Sixteen drams weigh 1 oz. Hence, a weight of 6-4-12 on the weigh board means 6lb 4 oz 12 dr (¾ oz).

If possible, walk along with the scalesman while he is weighing to check the catches of other anglers around you. If anyone has obviously fared better than the others, ask him what he did to give him that extra edge and make a mental note, or better still, a written one. It takes much effort, but a diary really is an indispensable aid to the match angler. In it you should record everything you think might be of value about every competition you fish – how you fared, how others fared, winning methods and pegs, time of year, water conditions, weather conditions and the like. It can prove more than helpful in future years. It's amazing what you forget unless you write it down. By offering to help the scalesman, you can ensure that you have a ringside seat when it comes to seeing the catches taken by other anglers.

Let's assume that you have fished many club events and have found yourself reasonably successful. The next step is an important one, and could make or break your match fishing career. You can do one of three things. First, you can stay in the same club, continuing to participate against the same anglers on the same venues and continuing to enjoy success. Or you may feel the time is right to join another club with new venues, new adversaries and new challenges. Finally – and this is the really big step – you might decide that the time is right to join the ranks of the open match anglers.

Your first open match can be a daunting experience. The chances are that many more anglers will be competing in this match than competed in the club matches you're used to. The odds of winning are considerably reduced and you will need to draw a good peg to stand a chance. Most open matches are on venues that have one or two noted pegs. On many occasions, unless you draw one of these, your chances of an overall win are slim. However, you can still win some money in an open event simply by attempting to win your section. Most open matches are split up into sections, often of 10 pegs in a line. The angler who wins his section can go home better off even though he didn't finish among the main prizes.

Others take an all-or-nothing approach. They fish every

When you hook a bonus fish like a chub, make sure you don't lose it!

open match to win as an individual, and often their chances of a section win are eliminated because of that. For example, many rivers in summer are dominated by bream and many open matchmen will fish exclusively for them, even though the nearest feeding bream shoal might be 50 pegs away. These rivers often contain good numbers of eels, certainly enough to provide a section-winning weight should the angler so desire. By fishing for eels rather than bream, however, an angler will almost certainly lose his chance of

Legering accounts for hundreds of match wins every season.

winning the match individually.

This is one of the reasons why the decision to enter your first open is such a big one. If you are serious about it, you will need the bait to cater for every eventuality, but the chances are you will take most of it home again with you. Fishing for your section is really like fishing a club match all over again, but in a team event such as a National Championship that is really all that you are doing. In fact, you might have to sacrifice your chance of individual glory for the sake of ensuring good points for the team.

Only you can decide upon your open-match approach. Knowledge of the venue helps, of course, and you should have some idea of the worth of the peg you have drawn before setting off to fish. Have you a chance of an individual win or even a top-six placing, or will you only be fishing for your section? If you have done your homework, you will have some idea yourself. But if you haven't and are fishing a venue that is relatively unknown to you, ask around after drawing your peg. You'll soon know if you're in with a chance by the looks on other anglers' faces . . . even if they don't tell you the truth. The rest is up to you. Perhaps a method at which you are proficient will be right for your section, but will give you no chance of winning the match from your peg. Then it would be wise to fish for your section and miss on the chance of individual glory. However, if you suspect, or have been told, that the match might be won from your area, it would pay you to throw caution to the winds and go for it. Fish too negatively on a good peg and you might waste your chance. Fish too positively on a bad one and you might miss out on a section win. The decision is yours.

21

CHAPTER TWO

TACKLE

••

Proper fishing tackle is one of the most important ingredients for match fishing success. That doesn't necessarily mean expensive tackle, but it does mean the right tackle. If you are to enter the world of match fishing seriously, there must be no half measures. You should never make the excuse that you didn't have the right tackle when you have failed in a contest. That's not to say that matchmen don't say exactly that many times a season, but why should you join them?

The right tackle means that you should have everything for the venue that you are fishing on a particular day. If your budget cannot run to different tackle for many different types of venue, it would be best to stick to the venues most suited to your equipment. Of course, much of your tackle will be perfect for numerous situations, and by choosing carefully you should be able to kit yourself out at the start of your match fishing career without breaking the bank. Much of the tackle that served you well during your pleasure-fishing days will suffice, especially if you owned a good pole and two or three different rods for floatfishing or legering. But what if you're starting from scratch? Here is a rundown of what you will need.

Floatfishing rods

Rods for floatfishing come in many different forms and you should think carefully before making your choice, ideally trying out several before buying. For all forms of floatfishing, look for a rod that is made from carbon fibre, or from carbon with some strengthening agent added such as whiskers of graphite or boron. Carbon has now well and truly taken over from glass fibre and its predecessors as it is altogether lighter, slimmer and has a better 'action'. The rod's action is the way it responds during casting, striking and playing a hooked fish. Floatfishing rods for match fishing, where small to medium-sized fish are usually the quarry, should have most of the action contained in the top and upper-middle sections of the rod. When big fish are expected, a rod with more power lower down into the lower middle and even the butt section might be required to steer them away from snags, although here you will need to use stronger tackle as well.

As for length, a rod of 13 ft is best. However, in the south of England, many anglers prefer 12 ft rods, even though the loss of 1 ft can pose problems when trying to control a stick float or a waggler in awkward wind conditions. With 13 ft, there is more carbon in front of your arm, allowing you to keep a more direct line to a stick float trotting through the swim, and when waggler fishing a 13 ft rod will 'pick up' line from the surface or beneath it faster than a 12-footer. This can be especially important when using a sunken line and allowing a bow to form as the line is blown by a downstream wind to enable a true passage of the float through your swim. You might need to pick up a considerable amount of extra line when you strike in these circumstances, and the extra foot can make all the difference.

For smaller waters – canals, some lakes, shallow drains – where shorter casts and lighter floats are required, many anglers prefer a shorter rod and with good reason. Where there is no advantage in a 13 ft rod, why use one? It's considerably heavier than one of, say, 11 ft, and this length can be used quickly and effectively all day. To a matchman, an 11 ft rod on a small water might mean a few extra small fish in the net at the end of the match, and those few extra fish could mean the difference between winning and finishing among the also-rans.

Of course, other lengths of rod are available, especially considering the 1992 World Championships on Northern Ireland's River Erne system. These were won by Italy using a method perfected on the River Po at Bologna. Called the Bolognese, the method involves the use of telescopic rods of up to 24 ft long and huge pole floats. It is a highly specialised technique only practical in conditions of favourable wind – back or slightly upstream – and deep water, preferably with a depth of over 15 ft.

Since the Italian victory, British match anglers have sat up and taken notice, and now you'll see a few Bolognese rods on the open-match scene. However, they don't lend themselves to the English weather. As they are telescopic, the rings are spaced well apart and line stick can be a problem in the wet when casting. In addition, they tend to be on the stiff side, and the small hooks and light hooklengths that are often required to catch fish in Great Britain are no match for most Bolognese rods. Breakages would be common. For this reason, some adventurous British rod manufacturers have introduced long, 20 ft take-apart rods so that the Bolognese method can be used successfully with British styles. The method has already won contests on the River Severn, and it could also be used to good effect on rivers such as the Yorkshire Ouse, Ure, Trent, Nene and Wye.

The best handles are made from cork, and when you're

23

The good match angler has everything to hand.

buying a rod, make sure the handle is not too long. The ideal handle protrudes 2-3 in from your elbow when you're holding it with the reel correctly positioned towards its front. Many rod handles are longer than necessary to give heavy rods better balance. By adding weight behind the arm, a top-heavy rod appears much less so. However, there really is no excuse for ultra-long handles on rods made from today's space-age materials.

Reel fittings are a small but important part of any rod. Undoubtedly the best are made from moulded plastic. Metal fittings can become very cold or very hot, whichever, they are uncomfortable. Good reel fittings should hold the reel firmly yet not so tight that it is difficult to fix the reel in place beforehand and to remove it afterwards. Some modern rods – and all Bolognese rods – have 'permanent' reel fittings that secure the reel by screwing it into place, a luxury that shouldn't be your only reason for buying a particular rod.

Rod rings come in many shapes and forms. For years, the simplest hard-chrome rings were the most popular, their lightness outweighing any weakness and their relatively short life-span. Many anglers still swear by them and indeed, good-

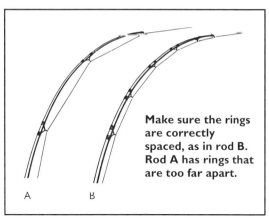

Make sure the rings are correctly spaced, as in rod B. Rod A has rings that are too far apart.

A   B

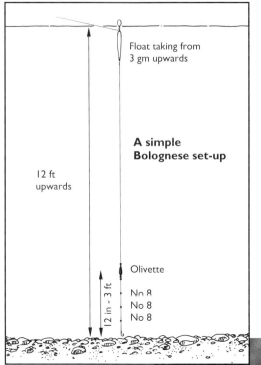

Float taking from 3 gm upwards

A simple Bolognese set-up

12 ft upwards

Olivette

No 8
No 8
No 8

12 in - 3 ft

Top left: Match rods should be powerful but forgiving.

Middle right: The Bolognese method is becoming more popular.

Right: Playing a big carp on match gear is a nerve-wracking affair.

quality, hard-chrome rod rings are difficult to beat, but they do need watching, and you might have to change them every closed season. Watch for tiny grooves where your line runs through the ring. As soon as these become apparent, the ring needs changing as breakages can occur easily, especially when a big fish is hooked and the line rubs against the sharp edges of the groove.

Look at the rings on most of the more expensive floatfishing rods and you will notice that they are lined with a material that is designed to be tough, friction-resistant and light. These lined rings are extremely popular and modern materials mean that they make very little difference to the overall action of a rod. Most rings have two 'legs', which are used to attach the ring to the rod, but technology has advanced even here, and some manufacturers are now using single-leg rings, especially on the tip section. It's on this light tip section that heavy rings have their most detrimental effect, so the lighter the rings, the better.

As for the number of rings on a floatfishing rod, there should neither be too few, nor too many. Thread a line through the rings of a rod and pull from the tip end. The line should follow the curve of the rod closely, not progress in a series of straight lines – a sure sign of too few rings. On a 13-ft rod, you should look for at least 13 rings, and more if they are of the very light type. The more rings you have, the heavier the rod will be, but line stick in the rain will be kept to a minimum – important when casting and trotting.

Whatever type of rings your chosen rods have, both butt and tip rings should always be lined. These two take a lot of 'stick', and plain hard-chrome rings are just not tough enough. The butt ring, or even the two rings nearest the rod's handle, should be larger than the rest, while those close to the tip can be smaller to save weight. Another point worth mentioning is that the butt ring should not be further than around 15 in from the reel. Further than this and 'wrapover' tangles are a potential problem, as well as line stick in the wet. However, if the ring is too near, it can impair casting potential.

How many floatfishing rods will you need? If you are to compete at the very top level, nothing must be left to chance, and there might be occasions when you will need to set up three or more float rods. They might all have different float set-ups, but they might even have the same. For example, in a really important match like a World Championships or even a National, anglers will have as many as a dozen rods set up beside them, many with identical rigs. Then, should a tangle occur, it's a case of dropping one rod and picking up another, perhaps making one or two small changes before you start fishing again. Tangles take time to undo, and time is the match angler's worst enemy.

Legering rods

Rods for legering come in even more varieties than those for floatfishing, with lengths from tiny, 6 ft 'wands' to rods for swimfeeder fishing, which might be 13 ft or more. Obviously, your choice depends on the type of venue you are fishing. Weight is not such an important consideration as it is with floatfishing rods, as the legering rod spends much of its time on the rod-rest, rather than held in the hand. However, carbon fibre's other qualities, such as strength and stiffness, are important when it comes to casting, striking and playing fish, so it's no surprise that carbon fibre is the most popular material for legering rods.

The matchman's main legering weapon is his quivertip rod, and there are a few things to watch for when making a purchase. The rod should be able to cast to the required distance, and remember that you might need to 'outcast' your rivals around you to catch more than them. Rods for long casts should have a good length – at least 11 ft – with enough power down through the middle section to 'punch' a leger weight or a swimfeeder. If the rod is too soft and sloppy, it will bend too much when you try to cast a good distance. However, rods for distance casting must be much more than stiff 'pokers'. For a start, you must be able to see your bites so a sensitive indicator has to be used at the rod tip. Try to choose a rod that provides at least two quivertips which are pushed inside or over the tip section, so that you can select the one that most suits the conditions on the day.

Altogether softer rods can be used for shorter distances, fishing with perhaps only a couple of SSG shot as the casting weight. Sensitivity is the key here, not only for spotting bites, but also for ensuring that the tip bends a little without pulling the light leger weight along the bottom. These rods should be up to 10 ft long, again with a choice of tips or, better still, with a couple of different complete top sections, so that the

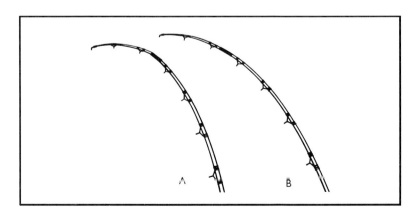

A bad splice (**A**) and a good splice (**B**). It can mean the difference between landing a fish and losing it.

quivertip is integrated with the rest of the rod rather than pushed into the end.

Rings on leger rods should be a little larger than those on floatfishing rods. This will ensure maximum casting potential, while the extra weight will not matter too much as the rod spends much of its time on the rests.

If you fancy swingtipping – and there is an increasing number of match anglers who do – look for a rod with a screw-in end ring and one that is fairly soft without being floppy. Such rods are appearing on the market more and more as swingtipping enjoys popularity once again.

Reels

Being a container for line, a reel holds the key to fishing distances beyond those attainable with line merely attached to the end of a rod or a long pole. By releasing line from a reel in the casting process, you can propel your tackle to a distance determined by several factors, including the weight of your float, leger, swimfeeder or bait, the type of rod, breaking strain of the line and, of course, how much there is on the reel spool.

Casting is the most basic function of a reel, but fixed-spool reels do much than that. Even after the tackle has reached the required distance and landed safely in the water, a reel allows float tackle to move with the flow along a river. This is the process known as trotting and necessitates the angler releasing line from the reel spool so that the float can continue its passage along the swim. Fixed-spool reels also help in the playing and landing of fish. Most are fitted with a drag system that can be adjusted to allow the spool to turn, releasing line to a running fish. The drag setting can be altered to allow for different breaking strains of line, big-fish anglers setting the drag so that it will operate just before the pull on the line is great enough to snap it. However, most match anglers do not use the drag system on their reels, tightening it fully and preferring to play their fish using the reel handle, winding and backwinding according to the fight of a hooked fish.

The first fixed-spool reels were introduced early in the 20th century, but not surprisingly they have progressed considerably since then. Now there are two types of fixed-spool reel, described as open-face and closed-face, and both have their uses to the match angler. Both open-face and closed-face reels have spools that do not revolve unless the drag system is being operated. The spool moves up and down during the normal winding and backwinding process and line is released or wound on by means of a bale-arm on the revolving drum (open-face) or pick-up pin on the

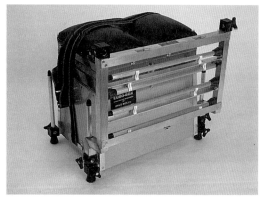

winding cup (closed-face).

How do you choose between an open-face and a closed-face reel? It all depends on what you want from your reel. Longer casts are usually possible with an open-face reel. Once line leaves the spool, there is nothing to hinder its progress towards the rod's butt ring. Although the extra distance possible would hardly be noticed when casting only 20 yd or so, the angler wanting to hurl a leger weight or swimfeeder 70 yd to a shoal of feeding bream would definitely be better off using an open-face reel. Recent top-quality reels of this type are able to cast even further thanks to special coned spools. The bale-arm mechanism is also more reliable than the line pick-up of a closed-face reel, and a revolving line roller on the bale-arm will help you to eliminate line twist.

Open-face reels do not suffer from a traditional closed-face problem of line 'bedding in', when the outside coils of line become trapped beneath those underneath. This manifests itself, usually after a sizeable fish has been landed, by the line and tackle 'catching' on the next cast. Gearing is usually smoother on open-face reels as well as stronger, and big-fish anglers would use one every time. They also have a faster retrieve, more line being wound back onto the spool for every turn of the handle than is the case with closed-face reels, and they are generally lighter.

Where do open-face reels fall down when compared to their closed-face counterparts? First, they can prove troublesome in rainy weather, as casting potential can be shortened once the line and spool gets wet. Wind is also a problem, because coils of line can be blown off the spool and become tangled in the other workings of the reel. Most problems occur when you're fishing into a head wind. Close control of line release when trotting with an open-face reel is not difficult, but it is easier with a closed-face reel, and the casting process can take a little longer because disengaging the bale-arm is usually a two-hand operation whereas with a closed-face reel it is a case of pressing in the front button.

Left: Make sure your reel is properly filled with line.

Right: Continental-style seat boxes are popular among match anglers.

29

However, open-face reels whose bale-arm can be released by a one-hand 'finger-dab' mechanism are available. Finally, after striking into a fish on a flowing river where you have been trotting through with the bale-arm open, it is sometimes awkward to engage the bale-arm without a little slack line being created. This can lead to lost fish.

Closed-face reels are unbeatable for delicate tackle control. After casting, you can control the passage of the float along your swim by 'feeding' line from the front of the reel between the thumb and forefinger of your left hand (if you are right-handed) or by simply pressing the line-release button, letting some line peel from the reel by moving your rod in an upstream direction, and then engaging the pick-up pins again by turning the handle slightly until you hear or feel the 'click' of the pins engaging. Repetition of the process will allow the float to travel along the swim in the 'stop-start' way that is sometimes so deadly. Casting with a closed-face reel is simplicity itself and can easily be carried out single-handed. All that you have to do is to push in the button at the front of the reel – there is no bale-arm. Engagement of the pick-up pins is also only a matter of turning the reel handle.

Closed-face reels have spools that are covered, avoiding damage to your line in the tackle box as well as preventing loops of line blowing around in windy conditions, and there are no jagged edges for line to catch against. Nor do many of them have any anti-reverse facility, as most anglers would never use it. However, line retrieve on closed-face reels is not as fast as it is on open-face reels; line 'bedding-in' can be a problem, although some modern closed-face reels claim to have eliminated this; and casting distance potential is not as great as it is with open-face reels. They are also generally heavier than open-face reels, and not as smooth running.

That is a quick summary of the advantages and disadvantages of open-face and closed-face reels. In practise, many anglers find that they prefer closed-face reels for close-in fishing with stick floats and other floats attached top-and-bottom, and for 'fast' fishing such as catching small fish on canals. Open-face reels are usually preferred for all other types of match fishing, including legering. Whichever type of reel you go for, make sure that it comes with at least two spools. This will allow you to use two different types of line, one sinking and one floating, for example, and make sure that the spools are correctly loaded with line. In the case of open-face reels, this means filling it to within $\frac{1}{16}$ in of the spool edge. With closed-face reels, you should wind on less line. Some top anglers claim that 75 handle turns of line on a closed-face reel is correct to avoid 'bedding-in', but you'll need to change line regularly otherwise you might find yourself with insufficient line on your reel after a time.

Luggage

There is a massive array of luggage on the market for match fishing, and what you choose should be determined by your requirements as well as your pocket. For example, a conventional English-style plastic seat-box will be perfectly adequate for the beginner to match fishing and could cost as little as £30. It consists of a container, a hinged lid, and a strap for carrying. However, more and more match anglers are turning to Continental seat-boxes because of their suitability and the way that they store delicate items such as pole winders. This type of box has an underneath compartment for large, bulky items such as reels, rod-rests and catapults, but incorporated into the lid are several drawers and trays that can be arranged to suit. For example, in one drawer you might want to store pole winders, in another wagglers and stick floats; and in another shot and small accessories. The permutations are many and varied.

Access to these trays and drawers is quick and easy, everything can be viewed at a glance, and some anglers even go to the length of buying two or more top compartments, which they stock up according to where they are fishing. They will have one for rivers and one for canals, for example, removing one from its hinges and replacing it with the other when the need arises.

Several British manufacturers now make these boxes from materials ranging from glass fibre to plastic. They tend to be heavier when empty than ordinary boxes, but with these new products you'll find that no extra tackle boxes are needed to store the more delicate items like floats, so their overall weight when full can be kept down.

Whichever seat-box you choose, make sure it has a padded seat cushion and, most important, adjustable legs. The match angler has to be comfortable when fishing, for comfort undoubtedly adds to his efficiency. Besides, if you're having to concentrate on staying seated on a sloping box, how can all of your efforts be put into the most important job of the day – catching fish? Your first job when you arrive at the waterside should be to gently place your seat-box where you want to fish, and adjust the legs accordingly.

The match angler will also need a good-quality holdall and carryall, the holdall for his rods and the carryall for bait, keepnet, landing net and bait trays. Matching sets can be bought, but don't fall into the trap of buying a larger size than you need. You will only fill them with tackle and bait that isn't required but that adds considerably to the weight you are carrying around. Make sure the holdall has three outside compartments, for banksticks, umbrella and pole, while the carryall should have an outside pocket for nets and trays.

31

Nets

A good-quality keepnet and landing net are musts for the match angler, and some even use different nets for different situations. For example, on a river or lake, a keepnet of at least 10 ft long will be required to ensure that the fish are in deep enough water, while on smaller waters and canals, a smaller net is often preferable as a large one can get swept around by wind, flow or wash from boats, and ruin your carefully fed close-in swim. Similarly, landing nets should be of an adequate size for the fish that you expect: large on a water where you expect bream or carp, but for small canal fish of perhaps only 3 oz or 4 oz, it would be a good idea to use a small net that you can manoeuvre easily, netting the fish almost as quickly as you would swing it from the water. An increasing number of anglers are turning to the new nets made from monofilament. These have been found to be kind to fish – especially when the bottom two sections are made from carp-sack material – do not smell, and dry quickly.

Other items

The well-equipped match angler will need to buy more than this if he is to compete properly with his rivals. A platform is a must. Buy one that houses your box comfortably and that has long legs with wider pads on the bottom to prevent it sinking into the mud. Make sure the leg-locking system is reliable and that the screws have good, sturdy knobs that are easy to grip. Once your platform is in place, leave it a few minutes to settle before checking it. You might find that you can tighten the screws a little more and that the platform sinks further into the mud. Only when you are happy that it is safe, should you place your box on it. Even if you don't use the platform for your seat-box, it can come in handy for somewhere to place your bait alongside you.

You will also need a pole and whips, and what you should look for is explained in the chapter on polefishing. Then there are all the accessories – floats for rod and reel and pole, pole winders, shot, hooks, groundbait bowls, riddles for maggots, line for pole rigs and hooklengths, good-quality keepnet and landing net with handle, banksticks, rod-rests, catapults (several), bread punches, pole cups, disgorgers, float rubbers, umbrella, bait-boxes, plummets, scissors, hook tier . . . and possibly a trolley to help carry everything along the bank! The list is a long one, but if you are serious about your match fishing, you will need to invest in the equipment to compete with the best.

CHAPTER THREE

FLOATFISHING

No coarse fisherman goes fishing without floats. They are the bread and butter of the art of angling, and when it comes to match fishing, the need for the right float is of paramount importance. Second best just won't do. All anglers, not just matchmen, get a thrill when that float slowly disappears beneath the surface; and when it does, we can in one sense be said to be masters of the art. We have, after all, convinced one fish at least that our bait is a natural offering that can be eaten without danger, and that's no mean feat. Of course, there is much more to floatfishing than this, and as you start to climb the match fishing ladder you will need to learn much about types and sizes of floats, and when you should use one particular float in preference to another for certain conditions on particular waters.

Before we embark on a detailed look at floats for match fishing, a word about lines. The best float in the world will suffer if the line to which it is attached is unsuitable. Don't go for pre-stretched lines for floatfishing. Their usefulness is restricted to polefishing and hooklengths. They simply do not have enough elasticity for use with rods, reels and floats. Instead, use a tried and tested line of around 2 lb breaking strain. A breaking strain of less than that will probably suffice for most of your fishing, if you choose one of the more abrasion-resistant lines, but in truth, you are unlikely to need to go finer than 2 lb.

You might sometimes want the line to float, at other times to sink, so it will also pay you to carry a small pot of washing-up liquid mixed with water (to make it sink) and some floatant spray (to make it float). You can then apply whichever you need to your spool before fishing. In favourable wind conditions, for example, you can keep the line on the surface easily without fear of losing control of your float tackle. However, in a wind, it will probably be best to use a sinking line, quickly achievable with a few drops of the washing-up liquid solution. If you have several different spools, take advantage of new lines that are being produced specifically to float or to sink. These new lines are excellent and can save valuable time and effort.

Now let's look at all the various floats you will need to compete successfully.

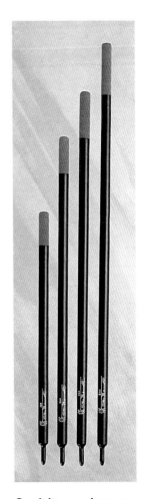

Straight wagglers are the most often used floats.

Straight waggler

The biggest-selling float around, straight wagglers account for hundreds of match wins every season. A straight waggler is a length of buoyant material that is sealed against water intrusion and has either a ring at the bottom or a peg for use with a float adaptor. Attached to line at the bottom end only and fixed in place by means of locking shot, wagglers are equally at home in running and still water, are most suited to catching on or close to the bottom, and are best made from peacock quill. The quills of peacock feathers are extremely light in weight as well as being straight and they make excellent floats.

The beauty of a float attached at the bottom end only is that the line between the float and the hook can be sunk beneath the surface if required, out of the way of any troublesome

The simplest of waggler rigs.

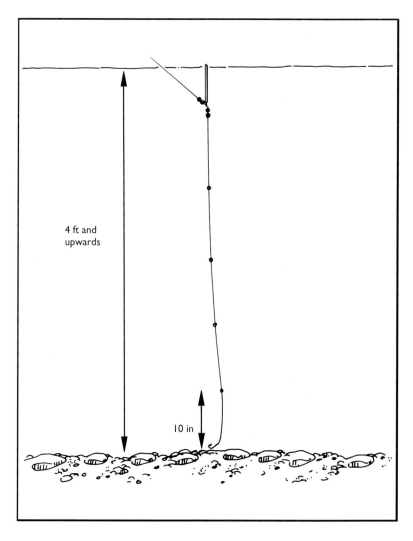

4 ft and upwards

10 in

wind. Whenever the wind is blowing, it affects the surface layers of the water. If you leave your line on the surface, it follows that the wind will affect that as well, blowing it around and pulling your float and bait unnaturally. If the rest of the water is behaving differently – that is, naturally – it follows that most fish will be suspicious of your bait.

However, if you sink the line between float and rod tip by dipping the rod tip under the water and making a couple of quick turns of the reel handle, you can achieve much better float control in unfavourable wind conditions. On flowing water, 'unfavourable' usually means that the wind is blowing in the same direction as the river current, making the top layers of the water skim along much faster than the true flow underneath. By using a straight waggler and sinking your line beneath the surface, you can minimise most of the effects of the wind.

You may still find that your line forms a bow between float and rod tip as the line is not being sunk enough to avoid the faster surface layers. Sometimes a longer float might be the answer, but it is more likely that you will have to 'feed the bow'. That means allowing a bow to be formed by letting line leave your reel as it is pulled out by the flow. If you don't allow this to happen, the float might be pulled along unnaturally fast. By 'feeding the bow', the float can trot through naturally. A sweeping strike is required when fishing like this because you have to pull a lot of line through the water before you connect with the fish. When conditions are more favourable, leave your line on the surface. The rule to follow is: keep your line on the top unless float control is adversely affected.

Straight wagglers come in many different lengths and thicknesses. The smallest floats might take only two No. 4 shot, and the largest four SSGs. The float you select should be determined by the weather conditions, the depth of the water and the flow. For example, in windy weather, you might need a heavier float to reach the required distance; in deep water, you might need a larger float to enable you to use more shot 'down the line' while still retaining enough casting weight around the float; and in waters with a fast flow, a thicker float will allow you to fish overdepth if you need to because the extra buoyancy in its tip will help pull the bait along the bottom. Look upon a float taking three AAA shot as the 'average' straight waggler and work from that.

Of course other materials are used for straight wagglers, such as sarcandas reed, balsa and even plastic. Clear plastic floats are popular in clear water on the assumption that they are less obvious to the fish. Whether or not this is the case is debatable, although man made material such as plastic is much more controllable than peacock quill, so it is easier to

35

Float adaptors make quick changes possible.

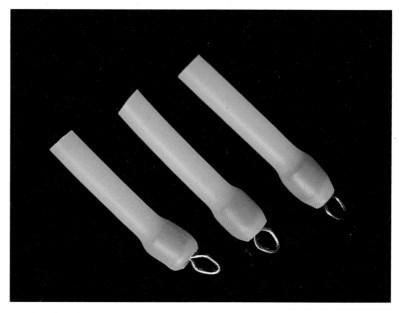

make the floats to an exact shotting requirement.

Finally, straight wagglers offer excellent visibility, so if you're fishing at long range, even in good weather conditions, you'll be able to see a straight peacock better than you will an insert waggler.

Insert waggler

In still and very slow-moving waters, in reasonable wind conditions, and when visibility is good, the best float to choose is the insert waggler. This type of waggler has a length of buoyant material as its main shot taker, plus a shorter length of material that acts as a sensitive indicator of a bite. The best insert wagglers are made from peacock quill with an insert of the same material. An insert made out of peacock will be buoyant, whereas one made from heavier cane will be less so, reducing the angler's options.

However, there are floats made from balsa wood or clear plastic that work almost as well. Insert wagglers are ideal summer floats. Locked on to the line by means of weights fixed either side of the bottom eye or float adaptor, the float should be as straight as possible to allow for pinpoint casting. Depth can be altered in seconds by moving the float up or down the line. It should also take plenty of shot for its size, hence the need for a highly buoyant material such as peacock quill.

Why the insert? The main reason for using an insert (of a thinner diameter than the main stem of the float) is the sensitivity required to spot bites from fish intercepting the bait as it falls through the water. It is a fact that fish – especially wary ones such as chub – will be suspicious of a bait that is hanging in front of their noses, but will take without hesitation one that is falling through the water. This is important to the matchman, who should always be on the lookout for a 'bonus' fish that will pull him up the prize list.

Often the best way of catching fish like this is to set the float so that the hook will finally settle off the bottom, but so that it will also fall through those fish that are feeding closer to the surface. Shot the float with most of its weight-carrying capacity locking it in place, and fix just a few small weights at equal distances between float and hook. The number of weights you use 'down the line' should be determined by the depth at which you are fishing. If you average one No. 8 per foot of depth, you won't be too far out. As you start the match, you should try to become aware of how long it takes the float to sink to its correct setting. If you are using an insert that is fine enough, you should be able to see the registration on the float of each individual shot. Any change to this routine and you can be certain that a fish has taken the bait.

Sometimes an on-the-drop bite will be unmistakable, the float diving away as the fish realises that something is amiss. However, just as often, the float will simply fail to settle properly as the fish takes the bait and stays in the same position, preventing some of the No. 8 shot from registering on the insert. Regular changes in depth are necessary to catch fish on the drop, especially in a match when a few minutes without a fish can be costly. Sometimes you will catch small lake carp by fishing only a couple of feet deep, while at others you might need to fish the full depth of the water. More often than not, when you're using an insert waggler, you are fishing for fish that not feeding not only on the bottom, but up in the water as well – and that water will not be very fast flowing.

Loaded waggler

When the use of most sizes of lead shot was banned several years ago, many float manufacturers started to produce loaded floats, with weights incorporated into the floats themselves. This meant that instead of using lead-weight alternatives – the early ones were not very good – anglers could shot the floats mainly with the still 'legal' lead No. 8s and smaller as dropper shot and perhaps a couple of non-toxic No. 1s locking the float in place on the line.

However, once this change was forced upon the angler, it soon became clear that there was a place on the market for loaded floats. Further developments were made and some of

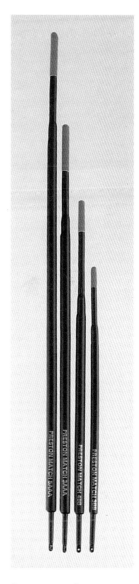

Insert wagglers are good for catching fish on the drop.

the more recent floats have special interchangeable weighted bodies allowing you to use different amounts of shot according to the size of the weighted body you attach. An obvious benefit to the match angler is the speed at which the size of float can be changed. Loaded floats cast very well as they tend to be streamlined, but one disadvantage is that they often plunge a good way under the surface, so should not be used in shallow water.

Loaded floats can also be used as sliding floats, and if anyone thought there was no place for sliders in match fishing, they should consider the 1992 World Championships in Ireland, won by Australian Dave Wesson using a sliding float. The method is limited to deep venues, and a loaded float is required to ensure that it stays resting against its stop shot during the cast instead of sliding up the line. Once the tackle has landed on the surface, the bale-arm of the reel

A sliding float rig.

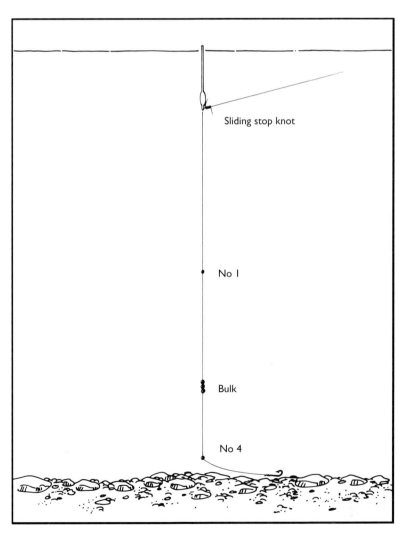

Sliding stop knot

No I

Bulk

No 4

should be kept open so that line can be released to allow it to slide through the float, which will eventually hit the sliding stop knot.

It's not a method that every match angler will need often, but it is worth carrying one or two loaded sliding floats in your box together with some tiny bottom eyes that are small enough to stop the float when it hits the sliding knot.

All-balsa waggler

Small wagglers designed for catching fish close to the surface and in shallow waters have been developed in recent years, and many anglers now prefer an all-balsa pattern for this type of work. Canal matches are often won using floats like these, their advocates claiming that they allow for faster fishing than the long pole as long as a bait presentation that is acceptable to the fish can be achieved. By casting these floats to various places around the swim, and not 'exhausting' any one particular spot, small fish such as roach can be caught all day long. Generous amounts of loose-fed squatts are usually required to keep the fish coming.

The matchman should carry a selection of these all-balsa wagglers taking from two No. 4s to three BBs. The best ones have short pegs at the bottom to house a float adaptor and a pronounced step at the bottom of the graded body. This acts as a brake once the float lands on the water, preventing it from plunging too far beneath the surface and possibly scaring fish feeding in shallow water. Larger all-balsa wagglers can also be used for catching fish feeding close to the surface on bigger waters. Dace, bleak and even chub can be taken in this way.

Bodied waggler

Bodied wagglers are rarely seen around the match circuit these days, but they do have their place and, as with sliders, it is worth the matchman carrying a couple around with him. They come in useful when a float carrying a lot of weight is required. A straight float might be too long and unwieldy to carry a lot of weight, but a bodied float can be a much more manageable size. Try them for bream fishing, with more shot than usual close to the hook to provide the stability this bottom-feeding species requires. This will still allow you to use enough weight around the float for ease of casting. The chances are, of course, that legering will offer a better alternative for a match-winning weight of bream, but you never know.

39

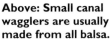

Above: Small canal wagglers are usually made from all balsa.

Middle: Stick floats are good for flowing water.

Right: Crowquill Avons are good in deep flowing swims.

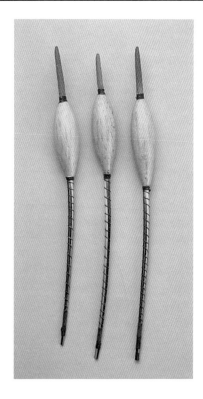

Stick floats

The match angler will need to make sure he carries a good selection of stick floats as well. These top-and-bottom floats can be truly deadly on their day and, fished properly, they can often outscore the waggler. Stick floats are floats for running water, designed with a buoyant balsa top part and heavier stem made from cane, heavy wood such as lignum, or plastic. They are usually fished with a floating line between float and rod top, although in awkward conditions with the wind blowing in a downstream direction, the line can be sunk and controlled with the help of one or two 'backshot' – small shot such as No. 8s that are fixed around 1 ft above the float to sink the line positively and out of the way of the wind.

The main limitation of stick floats is one of distance. They cannot be fished comfortably beyond a range of a few rod-lengths because control suffers unless the line between float and rod top is as straight as possible. As soon as any downstream bow is formed, the float is pulled off line and your bait will be ignored by most fish. In favourable wind conditions, control is much easier and greater distances can be explored, and there's no doubt that there are many times when a stick float will produce better than a waggler, even when they are fished in the same spot.

This is especially true when you're fishing for roach, and it really is worth the effort of setting up a stick float as well as a

40

waggler in flowing water. Modern materials make the task considerably easier. As well as the traditional stem of standard density cane, stick floats are also available with much heavier stems designed to help you cast further as well as providing better control in a wind. By casting a little way down your peg, and mending your line by lifting it and flicking it so that it does not form a downstream bow in front of the float, reasonable control can often be achieved even in seemingly adverse conditions. Sticks with wire or alloy stems are also good for riding boily water without being pulled around too much by the uneven current. Attach them to the line using three float rubbers: one tight one, ¼ in from the top of the float; a looser one in the middle; and a longer, ½ in one at the bottom that protrudes slightly over the end of the float. This will prevent tangles. Stick floats are available carrying from just a couple of No. 8s – designed for close-in work in warm weather for fish feeding in shallow water – to as much as eight BBs.

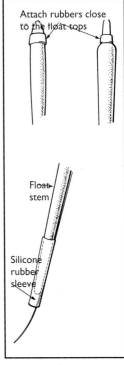

Above: Attaching a stick float to the line.

Left: A simple stick-float set-up.

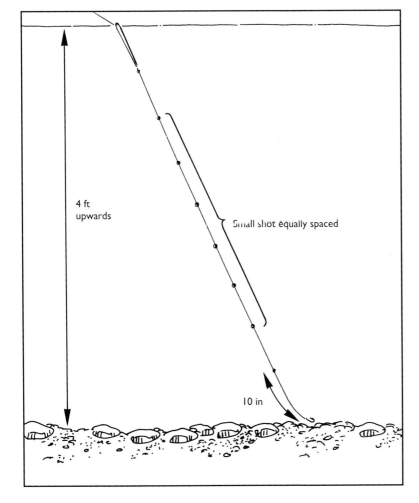

Crowquill Avon and balsa

Two more top-and-bottom floats that the match angler should carry with him on running water are the crowquill Avons and balsas. Both are designed to be fished with a bulk of weight close to the hook – either a string of BB shot or an olivette – and just one or two droppers underneath. They come in useful in deep, fast swims when you need to get your bait down quickly to the fish, and the crowquill Avon is also good in slower water that is affected by a strong upstream wind. While many floats would not be able to run through properly as they would be blown in the wrong direction, the bulk of the crowquill Avon is pulled through correctly by the flow close to the bottom. All-balsa patterns, meanwhile, will cast well and ride boily surfaces, making them ideal for swims where conventional stick floats might suffer. Another reason

A crowquill Avon rig.

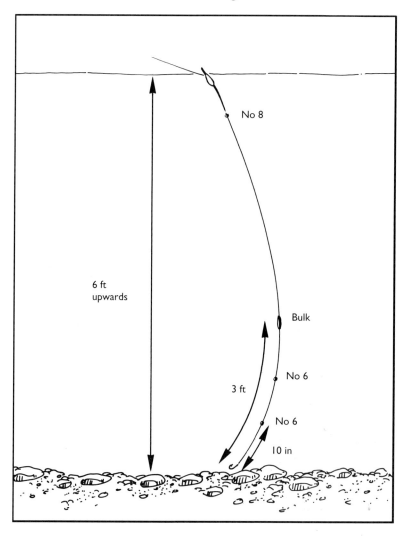

No 8

6 ft
upwards

Bulk

No 6

3 ft

No 6

10 in

for using both patterns is that their shotting means that your bait will be taken quickly through any small 'nuisance' fish feeding near the surface, down to the larger ones below. Of course, you might not want this if the anglers around you are struggling and you think that you can beat them with these small fry, but by catching larger fish closer to the bottom, you might have a chance of actually winning the match, and not just your section.

Tip colours and thicknesses

Make sure that you carry at least two identical patterns of every float in your box. There's nothing worse than building up a match-winning weight before suddenly losing or breaking your float and having to replace it with one that does not work as well. Make sure you have floats of different tip colours as well. The match might start in flat-calm conditions, probably making an orange-tipped float the easiest colour to see against the dark reflection of the far bank. Soon into the match, the wind gets up and suddenly the reflection on the water is lighter as the wind ripples the surface. Now you will probably need a black-topped float. Either you can change the float you are using, or you can quickly use a permanent black marker pen – something that no matchman should be without. A bottle of typewriter correcting fluid is also useful for changing float-tip colours from dark to light. Choice of tip colours is a matter for each individual angler. Many matchmen claim they can see orange best, whatever the reflections; others prefer yellow, while black is easy to see against light reflections. Black-topped stick floats are very important as you will usually need these when fishing fairly close to the bank, probably against the reflection of the light sky.

The thickness of a float's tip can also have an important bearing on its effectiveness. Obviously visibility is of prime importance – you have to be able to see the float – but it's equally necessary to use the right tip thickness for the type of fishing that you are doing. With wagglers, a thick, buoyant tip will allow you to drag some line along the bottom, especially if you undershot the float considerably to increase its out-of-water buoyancy, which will help pull the bait along. A thinner tip, meanwhile, will show on-the-drop bites better, as more of the tip will be pulled down into the water as each individual shot settles. With stick floats, a thinner tip will deflect the water when held back against the flow, preventing the float from being pulled too far above the surface, while a thicker, buoyant tip will keep its head above water even when the surface is a mass of boils.

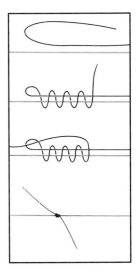

The sliding stop knot.

43

Adaptors

Most shop-bought wagglers come with bottom rings already attached, either as part of a plastic peg glued into the float stem, or whipped on to the bottom of the float. The matchman should not use them, but instead buy a few specially made float adaptors that allow a quick change of floats if the need arises without having to remove all the shot from the line and tackle up again. There are several types of adaptor available, and your choice should be governed by what float you are using at the time. Some floats have slim-diameter pegs at the bottom, while others are fatter. Use an adaptor whose internal diameter fits accordingly. Similarly, the bottom eye on adaptors varies. Some have half a swivel incorporated into them. If the swivel is small enough, this sort adaptor can be used pushed on to a loaded float to make a slider. Other types have a simple hole through a double layer of silicone rubber that has been melted together. These types are extremely popular and reliable, soft so that they do not damage line or float, and light in weight so that they do not take away much of the float's shotting capacity.

Clear plastic floats are best in shallow carp lakes.

CHAPTER FOUR

POLEFISHING

Anybody who goes match fishing seriously must have a pole. There's hardly a venue in Britain that has not seen at least one competition won by an angler using a pole. Even as little as 10 years ago this would have been ridiculous, but such has been the impact of the pole in recent seasons that it is now a necessary part of the match angler's armoury. On its day, the pole is unbeatable, for several reasons. First, much lighter tackle can be used than that required for rod and reel fishing at the same distance from the bank. This can be a great advantage on heavily match-fished waters such as canals

Big fish can be landed on the pole with a little care.

where delicacy of presentation is required. Second, in most conditions, a bait can be presented far more naturally to the fish with a pole than with any other type of fishing tackle. Third, many spots that would be inaccessible with a rod-and-reel set-up are fished comfortably and easily with a pole. A stretch of water underneath the trailing branches of an overhanging tree on the far side of a canal or small river might be out of bounds to the float or leger angler, but the pole angler can position his tackle perfectly under them.

The selection of your first pole is a real balancing act and there are many points to consider. On one hand are the qualities you need to look for - lightness, stiffness, strength, diameter and the right joints; set against these is the problem of affordability. The simple fact is that your pole is likely to be the single most expensive and valuable item of tackle that you possess. Good poles cost a lot of money, so even before you start to look for a pole, set yourself a budget, and don't even look at any poles that are beyond your financial means. It is worth saving until you can afford a pole that costs at least £300, preferably more. While a £200 pole will probably be comfortable to use at most lengths, beyond about 9 m it will start to become unwieldy and you will soon be wishing that you had a longer pole.

Eleven metres is the best length, although modern poles can be used at longer lengths than that, 17 and even 18 m have been reached by some pole anglers. Try to buy an 11 m pole if you can, and expect to pay anything from £200 to £2,000 for the privilege. You need spare top sections as well so that you can take them to the match fitted with different strengths and lengths of elastic according to the depth, size of float and size of fish you expect to catch. It is probably a good idea to visit one of the shops that stock a large selection of poles before making your choice. So what makes a good pole?

There are several things to be aware of. A pole that you want to use as an all-rounder should be as stiff as possible at its full length. Hold it still, flick it up and it should return to its original position quickly. Any beginner to polefishing will find even the lightest pole cumbersome to use at first. But after a few sessions spent mastering the holding and unshipping process, the importance of a light pole becomes apparent. The disadvantage with some light poles is that their strength is sacrificed. Thin walls are the problem. Check at the ends of each section. A gentle squeeze will be enough to tell. If the pole squashes more than a little, the chances are that it is too thin. Even the best poles in the world occasionally break, so before you buy yours, make sure that spare sections are readily available. Your tackle dealer will be able to tell you, and remember that you will need more than one top kit for different elastics as well. The best modern poles have joints that are described as put-over. This means that the sections nearer the pole tip fit over those nearer the butt. Poles with put-in joints have sections nearer the pole tip that fit inside those nearer to the butt. Most anglers prefer put-over joints.

Your new pole

Once you have brought your new pole home from the shop, you will be eager to get out on to the riverbank, but before that there are a few things you need to do. The first is to fit elastic into the top one or two sections. Elastic is a must when using a long pole, as it is your only insurance against a big fish. Acting as a shock absorber, elastic is fitted inside the pole tip to come into play when a fish is hooked. The tips on long poles are stiff, and it's easy to 'bump' even small fish if you're not using elastic. Once hooked, a small fish can be brought safely to the bank without the elastic having to do too much work. You might not even see it being pulled out from the inside of your pole tip. However, if you hook a larger fish, you will see the elastic being pulled out from the pole tip as the fish pulls against you. The more the elastic stretches, the more pressure it is exerting on the fish, which will eventually tire and can be brought to the landing net. Of course, things don't always work as smoothly as that. It is crucial to choose the right elastic. If you use elastic that is too fine and you hook a large fish, the fish will soon pull it to its maximum stretch – described as 'bottoming out' – and probably snap your line or, worse still, your elastic. On the other hand, if your elastic is too thick and you hook small fish, you might lose them when you lift the pole after getting a bite because the force of the elastic expanding and then contracting pulls the hook into the mouth and out again just as quickly.

Fitting elastic into your new pole is not difficult, but if you're unsure, get your tackle dealer to help you. You may need to saw a few inches off the pole tip so that a friction-free PTFE bush can be fitted, and you will also need a plug or bung for securing the other end of the elastic in either the first or second section of the pole. You should decide how long you want the elastic according to the size of fish you are expecting to catch. For example, if your match is on a water where small fish are the quarry, a fine elastic secured only through the top section will be fine, but if you are fishing where larger fish can be expected, it would be prudent to thread thicker elastic through the top two sections of your pole. Set it on the slack side initially just in case the big fish aren't feeding and to ensure that you don't 'bump' too many small fish. You can always tighten it later by either cutting an inch or two off one end of the elastic or, better still, by using a special elastic tensioner, a short length of plastic with a hook at both ends. You simply pull the bung out of the end of the second section bringing the elastic with it, wind some of the elastic around the tensioner, and secure it at both ends in the hooks.

There are several ways of connecting the tip end of the

47

**Belgian maestro
Marcel van den Eynde
is a master at pole
fishing.**

elastic to the line. Most popular is the Stonfo Connector, a small, black plastic device to which are attached both elastic and loop at the end of the line. However, some top matchmen have turned to a neater and just as reliable way of attaching line to elastic. It involves simply threading 1/4 in of narrow, stiff tubing up the elastic, then tying a small loop in the end of the elastic and cutting it so that you're left with three 1/2 in stubs. On the end of the pole-rig line are two loops, a large one, with a smaller one tied on the end of it. Now you simply reach through the large loop in the line, pull the rest of the loop through, drop the end of the elastic through this new loop and tighten behind the knot in the elastic, before sliding the tubing over the knots to neaten everything up. To remove at the end of the match, simply slide back the sleeve and pull sharply on the smaller loop.

Floats

Floats for polefishing are generally totally different from those required for rods and reels, the main reason for the difference being that pole floats are dropped and not cast into the swim. Obviously this means that no actual casting weight is required to propel the tackle to the swim. Any weights that are fixed on to the line are done so to present the bait in a certain way, to cock the float and to combat the wind. Most pole floats look very different, too, and most of the wagglers and stick floats you have lovingly collected will be useless for polefishing. The majority of pole floats have a length of very thin material protruding from the top of the body, which makes possible the finesse offered by the method – a fine bristle could rarely be used for rod- and-reel fishing because good tackle control and visibility would be impossible. However, when you're polefishing you can enjoy good control while still maintaining delicate bait presentation. The bristle serves as a means of bite detection and as long as the right shape and type of float body is used, properly weighted so that the whole of the body is beneath the surface, perfect tackle control can be achieved with ease.

The way you attach pole floats to the line is also different. Unlike wagglers and stick floats, most pole floats have a tiny wire ring glued in near the top of the body. The line goes through this first, then through one or two short lengths of soft silicone rubber on the stem of the float – one just beneath the body, the other at the bottom end of the body, protruding slightly over the end. Take care when choosing pole-float sleeves. Some are made from hard plastic and this can soon damage delicate wire or cane stems.

Bristle materials can broadly be split into three – plastic, cane and wire. A few floats have bristles made from carbon or even glass fibre. Most popular bristle material is plastic, which can be coloured so that it is fluorescent, and can be made in varying thicknesses. Cane, meanwhile, is more buoyant and useful for spotting bites before the bait settles. A wire bristle is the most sensitive of them all as it contains no buoyancy at all, wanting to sink at the slightest opportunity. Many top

Left: Fit your elastic with great care.

Right: Many anglers take dozens of pole rigs with them.

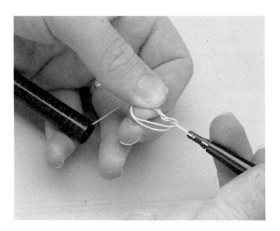

pole anglers like to use wire bristle for shy fish, claiming they register bites that would not be seen on other bristles. Some pole floats do not have bristles at all, but merely a continuation of the balsa body. These can be useful on rivers, or in situations where a bristle is difficult to see properly.

Pole float bodies come in many shapes and sizes, and your choice should be determined mainly by two factors – flow and wind conditions. Add to these depth when choosing the size of the pole float you want. As a general guide, the faster the flow, the more squat the pole-float body should be, with a 'shoulder' towards the body top. In waters with no flow, a float with a long, slim body can be used, as long as the wind is not too strong. The most stable pole float in windy conditions is one with a long, almost parallel balsa body and long wire stem, or a float with a more squat body whose fattest part is towards the bottom of the body. A combination of two of the body shapes mentioned gives the ideal one for windy conditions on a flowing river – just about spherical.

Like pole-float bodies, stems are available in several different materials including wire, cane, carbon and glass fibre, but the beginner to match fishing with a pole should stick to the floats he knows best and has been using for the most time. These will probably have stems made from wire or cane. Wire is the most stable material, and is ideal for fishing with a bait close to the bottom as it helps the float settle upright quickly. Cane, on the other hand, is sensitive and tilts as the shot settle. For this reason it is a good material for a float used for catching fish at all levels in the water with strung-out weights as opposed to a bulk. Bites are easy to spot if there is any change to the usual tilting of the float. Cane stems are also best for floats used when fishing 'to-hand'; in other words, with a length of line that is the same as the length of pole you are using. This is because wire-stemmed pole floats have a habit of spinning and tangling when swung out on a long line to the water. Length of stem varies according to the size of float, but you need a stem long enough to give the float stability. In windy conditions it follows that you will need a float with a longer stem than you need in calm conditions.

Manufacturers mark the side of pole floats in two different ways. On some they tell you what the float takes in grams, while on others they give the float's capacity in styl weights. The smallest pole floats take perhaps three or four No. 7 styls, while the largest carry 20 g. For most of the polefishing you will be doing during a normal match-fishing season, you will need a selection taking ¼-2 g. As they are very delicate items, great care and a good deal of time has to be taken when shotting pole floats, and for this reason most matchmen do the job at home. Not only can they be certain of obtaining exactly the right shotting every time, they are also saving themselves valuable time before the start of a match. To some, making their own pole rigs becomes an obsession and you might find more than 100 ready-to-use pole rigs in their box, all stored on special winders in trays specially made for the job. Others prefer to use just a few favourite rigs, changing the line regularly. You, too, must make sure that you are well prepared, whichever category you fall into. The well-prepared pole angler need have no worries about whether he has the right kit when he arrives at the waterside. Everything should be in its place, with the homework done beforehand.

So how do you set about making up a pole rig? First you have to decide what tackle you require. Line length is important, depending on the depth and flow of the water. On stillwaters, the ideal length of line between float and pole tip is around 1 m, so if the water is 2 m deep, that means a total line length of around 3 m between hook and pole tip. On rivers with some flow, more line will be required between float and pole tip to allow the float to travel further along the swim. In windy conditions, you will also need more line between float and pole tip so that when the pole is blown around, it doesn't pull the float with it, ruining your bait presentation. Pole rigs must also be of a length so that when you unship the pole, you can swing a fish safely to hand or net it without having to reach up or down, which takes up valuable time and might even result in a lost fish – a disaster for the matchman.

The best way of making sure that the rig length corresponds to the desired length of pole is to set the pole up and measure the line alongside it at home before breaking the line and wrapping the completed rig round a winder. Some top anglers make all of their rigs of a certain type to the same length, regardless of where they will be fishing. Then they alter the length once they have arrived on the bankside and plumbed the depth, either by removing or adding line at the top of the rig. On the subject of line, many modern high-tech lines are suitable for polefishing, but if you are not confident in using them, stick to the reel lines you know well. However, it would pay you to use line of a little less breaking strain than you would on the reel.

As for weights, the pole angler has a choice of three types. When the intention is to fish on or close to the bottom for the whole match, you would be better off using an olivette rig. The olivette is a streamlined, almost tubular weight through whose centre the line is passed. It is prevented from sliding all the way down to the hook by a small shot a No. 8 or a No. 10 fixed on to the line where you want the olivette to sit. They are available in sizes from 0.1 g to more than 15 g, and between the olivette and the hook you should fix one or two small shot or styl weights called droppers Match anglers would also do well to secure the olivette above as well as below, otherwise the weight will slide up towards the float every time you bait up or unhook a fish.

An increasing number of pole anglers are turning to conventional, round split shot to weight their pole floats. Shot are certainly the simplest way of setting a float and anglers like them for their versatility. Unlike an olivette, several shot fixed on to the line to form a bulk can be separated to turn the rig into one where the weights are strung out, resulting in a different kind of bait presentation. For most polefishing situations, it is best to use no shot larger than No. 8.

Finally, many pole anglers and most Continental matchmen use styl weights to shot many of their pole floats. These cylindrical weights are fixed on to the line with special pliers and they offer the most delicate presentation of the bait imaginable. With care they can be moved up and down the line to make bulk or strung-out rigs, and sizes of concern to the match angler are No. 12 (largest) to No. 7 (smallest). By separating a group of styls or shot, you can keep in touch with fish if they change their feeding habits by moving up in the water to intercept the bait as it falls. This is important if you are to get the most from a swim containing small fish, where a few minutes without a fish can prove costly.

Making rigs

Some matchmen like to make up all of their pole rigs before the start of the season, while others prefer to do a few, if required, before each match. The second way is best. You know exactly where you will be fishing and you can be certain that the line is fresh and won't let you down just when you hook that all-important bonus fish. Making rigs at home is a simple task that can be carried out with the help of a special neutral- buoyancy device for shotting pole floats. Push the float into a locating point in the float shotter and add weights to the saucer around it. By testing the float in a bucket of water you will soon reach the correct shotting – only part of the bristle should be showing – after which you can measure out the length of line you require against your pole, thread the float on to the line, and fix the weights underneath. Then it's just a case of wrapping the completed rig around a pole winder, secure it with an elasticated pole anchor, and write on the side of the winder any details that you consider to be important, such as line strength or diameter, line length, and the date the rig was made.

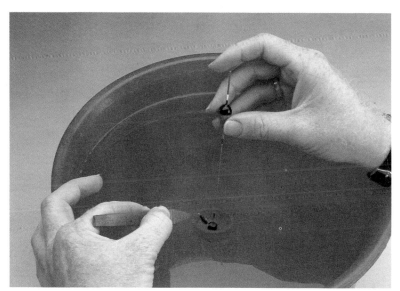

Styl weights are attached to the line with special pincers

Make up three or four rigs before each match and you will soon have a boxful, but try not to use one rig more than about three times. If you really like it – and we all have favourite floats – you should make it up again frequently. Another way of making up rigs at home is to fix the float and weights on to the end of a measured line and test the floats in a deeper container of water, such as a plastic lemonade bottle with the narrow top cut off.

Using a pole

A pole certainly takes a bit of getting used to, but once you have got the hang of it, you will wonder what all the fuss was about. The biggest sticking point for beginners to polefishing is the process known as shipping and unshipping. These are the terms used to describe the act of adding sections to the pole to take your end tackle out to the water, and removing them to land a fish, check your bait or change depth and shotting pattern. Unshipping begins once a fish is hooked. Strike gently with an upwards lift of the pole and try to assess the size of the fish before starting to feed the pole back through your hands. If it's a large fish, you might just need to hold the pole for a few seconds to allow the elastic to take the strain; but if it's a small fish you can begin unshipping immediately.

Look behind you and push the pole through your hands, resting it behind you on a suitable surface, until you reach the joint where the length of the pole in front of you equals the length of line you are using. Once you have reached the right joint, swiftly pull the pole apart and rest the section of the

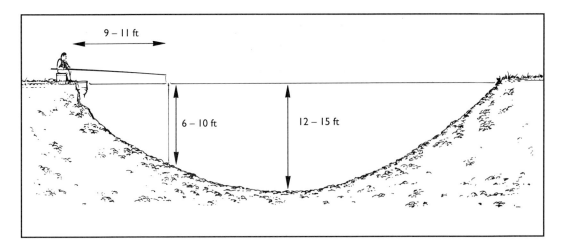

9 – 11 ft

6 – 10 ft

12 – 15 ft

Many large canals are shaped like a basin.

pole behind you on the ground, in the mouth of the keepnet, or in a special protector that is available from tackle shops. Anywhere will do, just as long as the pole doesn't slide into the water. After unshipping, check that the fish is still hooked – you should be able to feel it or, if it's bigger, you will see the elastic coming out from the pole tip – and either swing it to your hand or net it as required. You will find that you naturally swap hands to do this, and soon you will be unshipping in seconds. Simply reverse the procedure to take your tackle out to the water, lifting it at the last moment and laying it on the surface so that your bait falls in an attractive arc down to the fish.

Whips

For speed fishing when large numbers of small fish can be expected, the matchman should go armed with a whip. These are poles fitted with fine solid carbon flick-tips instead of elastic, and are fished 'to-hand', ie, with a line of the same length as the whip. There is nothing faster for catching close in, as long as you can control your tackle well enough. Sometimes you might need to use a small waggler, sinking the line after flicking the tackle out between whip tip and float if it's windy. For top-and-bottom fishing, use slightly larger floats than you would for short-lining, with an olivette or bulk to give you casting weight, and either swing the tackle out underarm, or flick it over your head. Whips start at 2 m, but in practice you will hardly ever need one that's less than 3 m. A fairly recent addition is the partly telescopic and partly take-apart whip. This allows you fish at, say, 4 m to hand, with the option of adding sections later in the match as the fish move out, as often happens when the shoal is reduced in numbers and the fish become wary.

CHAPTER FIVE

LEGERING

∙∙

There are many ways in which a match can be won, but ask most matchmen what method they used to take their biggest match weight, and the chances are that it was by legering. Legering offers the match angler a real opportunity of putting together a big weight of fish. So do other methods of course, but where big fish – especially bream – are the quarry, there is rarely anything to beat legering. The placing of a bait on or very close to the bottom is the best way of catching this bottom-feeding fish, and once you catch one bream, the chances are that others will follow. Bream are shoal fish, and as long as you don't do anything stupid, there is no reason why many more should not come to the net. Despite what some anglers will tell you, legering is not a lazy man's way of fishing. They claim that it is nothing more than a 'chuck it and chance it' method, doomed to failure more often than not, and nowhere near as skilful as other forms of match fishing. Such claims are way wide of the mark. On its day, legering is an unbeatable way of amassing a match-winning bag, and it's just as much an art form as other methods. The matchman who doesn't include legering as part of his repertoire is sadly mistaken, and the chances are that he will miss out on some great opportunities to make a name for himself.

However, legering is not just about big weights. At times it can be the only way of catching fish – any fish – and this can be of vital significance in an important team match decided on section points. That 'desperation' ruffe caught legering might lift your team from nowhere to the medals. It also serves as an excellent secondary way of tackling a swim that you would normally floatfish. Cast a leger weight or small swimfeeder to a shoal of roach and you may well catch one of the shoal's larger members. These naturally wary bigger specimens might soon become used to a bait presented on float tackle, but when something different suddenly appears, such as your legered bait, they will take it without hesitation.

Nor is legering restricted as to where it can be used. If more anglers legered in canal matches far fewer big carp would be lost, and much bigger winning weights would be taken. But this is all part of the match angler's dilemma. Should he sit it out waiting for one fish that could win the match, or should he plug away with the smaller ones? They're more reliable,

Legering accounted for this fine match catch from Yorkshire's Castle Howard Lake.

but by pursuing them he might miss his chance of glory. In a team event, of course, there is no real choice to make. He must fish for the team, and that means catching fish. However, if he feels he has done well enough after an hour or two, there should be nothing to stop him trying to catch something much bigger, especially if he is on a swim where big fish are known to live.

One common way of trying to do this is to feed for big fish in one area of the swim and for small fish in another, usually close to the bank, and to start off by fishing for small fish before moving out for the bigger ones later on. This serves two purposes. It ensures that you fulfil the match angler's, and especially the team angler's, requirement of putting something in the net, and it gives the larger fish, if there are any, time to 'get their heads down' on your feed. On a canal, this feed might be several catapult pouchfuls of hemp and casters for carp and chub; on a drain or river it might be loose-fed casters for bream. And the chances are that if and when you do decide to try your hand for the bigger fish, the best method will be legering.

So what are the advantages of legering over floatfishing? Most obvious is that it gives you the chance to offer a static bait to the fish. This is hardly ever possible when floatfishing with a rod-and-reel set-up as the slightest breeze will have some effect on the water and make the tackle drift around. A static bait will often appeal to bottom-feeders like bream, and there are times when all fish will ignore any bait unless it has been lying on the bottom for some time. This is especially common in cold weather when most fish are unwilling to feed at all. Eventually, one will take a legered bait simply because it is there. It might be the only bite you get and the only fish you catch, but who cares if it's a match-winning 3 lb bream or a 6 lb carp?

The nearest that you can come with float tackle to ensuring a static bait is to use a pole, and here we can immediately see another great advantage enjoyed by legering over floatfishing – distance. If you want to cast a long way, the best bet is to leger. On big waters, the biggest fish often stay well clear of the banks, so you will need to cast to them to stand a chance of catching one. Legering is the way. However, don't assume that legering can only be used with static baits. There are ways to make a legered bait move around attractively in a completely different fashion from the way a floatfished bait moves, and that might just be the way of catching on a particular day.

Weights

The match angler's favourite type of leger weight is undoubtedly the Arlesey bomb, and not without good reason

Carry a variety of leger weights with you.

A simple open-end feeder set-up.

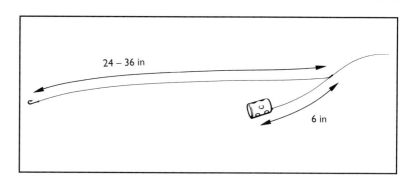

Arlesey bombs are streamlined, cast well, hold the bottom well, but pull away easily when it's time to reel in, and are available in all the sizes you're ever likely to need. They start at around ⅛ oz, and the matchman should carry a selection of Arlesey bombs from this size up to 1 oz. Heavier weights are available, but these should be considered only in exceptional circumstances – to hold bottom in flooded rivers, for example. Carry at least two of each weight so that, should you lose one, you can quickly replace it with another of the same weight. Choose Arlesey bombs that have rounded bottom ends, neither pointed nor quite flat. Both the latter will cause disturbance when entering the water, not a problem in deep water but potentially disastrous in shallow water.

The weight of bomb that you use should be determined by distance and flow. You need a leger weight that you can cast comfortably to the spot where you want it to land. Choose one that is too light and you will never be consistent in your casts with the slightest wind blowing the weight off course. Choose one that's too heavy and you are simply 'wasting' weight as well as risking scaring the fish in shallow water, unless you need a heavier weight to allow you to hold bottom properly. On flowing water, it's worth remembering that you will need less weight to hold bottom if you cast a little downstream between you and your neighbour than you will if you are casting directly in front of you. This is because the full force of the flow can push against the line if you cast in front of you, whereas it pushes more along the line when you cast downstream. When casting downstream, fish with your leger rod pointing in front of you so that there is a right angle between the tip of your rod and the line.

Of course, there are many other weights available to the leger angler, but most match anglers even use Arlesey bombs when trying to catch fish in flooded or partly flooded rivers, although one trick many employ in this situation is to use a flattened Arlesey bomb. These tend to hold the bottom better than ordinary weights. There is one other form of weight for the line when legering, and it can be highly successful on its day. That is to use one or more round split shot, just enough to hold bottom on a dropper of around 6 in. By changing the size and number of weights from No. 4s to SSGs, you can make the bait behave in many different ways. Combined with regular 'twitches' – lift the rod and give a gentle pull so that the weights and bait are moved a little along the bottom – these can provoke fish into feeding that would otherwise have ignored anything you could offer them.

Quivertip or swingtip

There are only two forms of bite detection for legering that the matchman need consider. These are the quivertip and the swingtip. Both attach to the end of the leger rod, and both serve similar purposes: they move when a fish takes the bait. Quivertips are by far the more popular of the two, although swingtips have enjoyed something of a revival in recent years, especially when bream are the target. A swingtip is a length of nylon, cane, carbon, glass fibre, or any relatively heavy material, attached to the end of your leger rod by means of a screw attachment and a shorter length of flexible rubber. The swingtip hangs down from the rod tip, and after you have cast out and correctly adjusted the line, it will rise or perhaps drop back when a fish takes the bait. Unless you buy a swingtip rod with a tip already whipped on to the end, you will need a rod with a special threaded tip ring attached to the end. On the other hand a quivertip is effectively an extra-sensitive extension of the rod tip. It bends or just quivers when you get a bite. Quivertips can be bought with screw attachments for fixing on to the end ring of a leger rod or with various push-on tips, or you can buy a special rod with the quivertip spliced into the top section. Some rods have several top sections allowing you to choose the best quivertip for the day.

Before you discount the swingtip in favour of the quivertip, just take a look at a few of its advantages. First, it can be fished with the rod in any position. If you are sitting on an open bank, you can position the rod anywhere from parallel with the bank to the left or right of you, to pointing straight out in front of you. This allows you to place yourself in the most comfortable position – important if you are to be as efficient as possible. A quivertip angler doesn't enjoy such freedom. A quivertip rod needs positioning roughly at right angles to your line after you have cast for the tip to be at its most sensitive. With your rod pointing straight out in front of you, a quivertip is useless unless you have cast well downstream in flowing water. Whichever tip you use, you will usually do best to position the rod so that the tip is almost

59

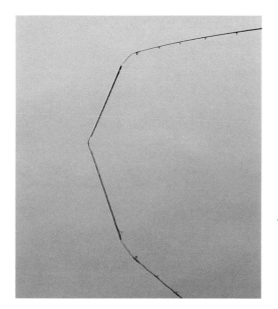

Above: Swingtipping is regaining its popularity.

Right: Choose the right quivertip to ensure you spot every bite.

touching the surface of the water.

Another advantage of the swingtip is that it shows you how a bite is developing much better than a quivertip can as it seems to magnify the movement, allowing you to wait until you are convinced the time is right to strike. Along similar lines, when a quivertip is pulled as a fish takes the bait, its tension increases, resulting sometimes in the fish dropping the bait as it suspects something is amiss. With a swingtip, this does not happen – the tension remains the same throughout the bite until the rod top starts to bend, by which time you have struck anyway!

If there are these advantages to using a swingtip, why do most matchmen still prefer the quivertip? Simply because a quivertip is easier to use – a quivertip adjusts itself to the effect of the current or wind.It is also preferable in a wind because a swingtip gets blown around much more, and because it is much easier to cast long distances than a swingtip, which is prone to wrapping around the rod tip and impairing distance. Finally, a quivertip can be used in flowing water, whereas a swingtip loses most of its effectiveness as it is pulled out by the flow.

Whichever type of tip you choose, you will need to make sure that your leger rod is as stable as possible while you are fishing. Do this by positioning at least two rod-rests, one no closer to the tip of the rod than 2 ft and one closer to the butt, ensuring that the rod does not 'sag' between the two! You can rest the rod butt con your upper leg, or you can use another rod-rest for the butt. The leg method is better as the rod is closer to hand and you can fish easily with your striking hand 'poised' over the handle. The important rod-rest is the one nearest the tip. Use one with several notches to allow you to position the rod in several positions to obtain just the right tension on the tip. These notches will also prevent the rod from sliding around in the wind. A target board is also a must for a matchman after a weight of fish on the leger. This is simply a plastic or wooden square measuring around 10 in – round ones are also available, though not as good – which screws into a bankstick and should be positioned so that you can 'read' the tip of the rod against it. It is useful in windy conditions when you would otherwise be watching the tip against the ripples, or when the fish are biting without hardly moving the tip. Bites such as these are surprisingly frequent from fish that are feeding confidently, as they pick up the bait and very slowly move away to find the next morsel, or even stay where they are. So-called 'sailaway' bites are usually made by nervous fish that take the bait and dart off immediately. They might also be line bites, caused by fish catching the line with their fins or body. Line bites can be a nightmare to the matchman and they can be very difficult indeed to distinguish from proper bites. The problem is that by striking at too many line bites, you might eventually scare the fish away. Many a match-winning peg has been wasted because the angler struck at line bite after line bite, eventually scaring a bream shoal before it had even settled down to feed. One trick if you are getting bites that you suspect are line bites is to twitch the bait. You can do this in several ways: by pulling on the line between reel and butt ring until you feel the weight move; by lifting the rod and pulling back on it until you feel the weight move; or by simply winding in with the rod in position until you feel the weight move. With all three you will probably need to tighten up again after twitching. Watch very carefully as bites can come straight away.

Tails and droppers

The best way of arranging your end tackle when legering with an Arlesey bomb or split shot is to use a tail and a dropper – otherwise known as a paternoster rig. It involves tying a short length of line some distance away from the hook and tying the Arlesey bomb or fixing split shot on this short length. Six inches is the norm, and to be honest, this dropper length is not too important. Of much more importance is the length of the tail – the distance between the dropper knot and the hook. Three feet is the standard length, but if you find that you are missing bites, or not seeing them, it is worth shortening it. Conversely, if some bites are coming very quickly after casting out, the chances are that some fish are feeding way off the bottom. By increasing the tail length, you

61

will be giving your bait more time to fall after the leger weight has hit the bottom. Watch carefully and you might spot bites while it is falling. The best way of attaching dropper to tail is by using a four-turn water knot and attaching the weight to the free end that points down from the knot – not up, as this end of the knot is the weaker of the two.

Swimfeeders

Love them or loathe them, swimfeeders are a vital part of the match angler's equipment. They have accounted for hundreds of match victories with most coarse fish species, but especially bream, barbel and chub, their great benefit to the angler being that they ensure that your hookbait is lying alongside some other feed that has been carried out into your swim in the feeder. Two basic types are available – blockend for loose maggots or casters, and open-end for groundbait. Both carry bait to the bottom where it disperses out, attracting fish to the area immediately around your hookbait.

There are many variations on the two main types of swimfeeder, with some tiny blockends carrying just $\frac{1}{8}$ oz of weight. These can be used on hard days when bites are at a premium, or to ring the changes on a swim that you have been floatfishing. Larger blockends carrying more weight are used in flowing rivers, and some huge weights of chub and barbel can be taken by match anglers introducing as much as 1 gal of maggots during the course of a five-hour contest. Extra clip-on weights are available to ensure the feeder stays put on the bottom in fast-flowing water. Such situations

Open-end feeder fishing is good for bream in competitions.

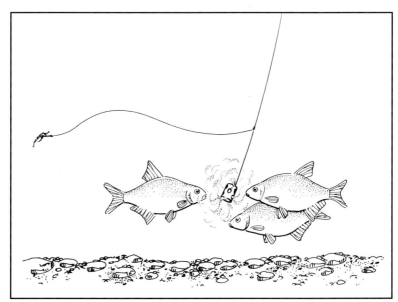

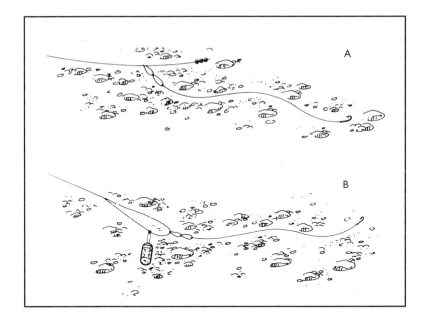

Two ways for flowing water.
A – link leger.
B – blockend feeder.

should be tackled with a rod of at least 11 ft long, and after casting you should use a special rod-rest to ensure that the rod tip is pointed up in the air, unlike other forms of legering. This is to keep as much line as possible out of the water, otherwise it would be pushed by the flow, necessitating the use of a heavier, and less sensitive, feeder.

Open-end feeders are favoured by anglers fishing for bream, the feeder being filled with a dryish mix of groundbait containing loose offerings such as casters and squatts. Most open-end feeders are made from plastic with a lead strip along the side, although more specialised open-ends are made from wire mesh, which is heavier for longer casts, more robust and allows the feeder's contents to be released quickly.

Smaller and lighter feeders can be attached to the line in the same way as ordinary leger weights, using a simple paternoster rig. However, such set-ups will not be strong enough for larger and heavier blockend feeders. These are best used sliding along a large loop to help absorb some of the casting and striking pressure, as well as forming a rig similar to the carp angler's bolt rig. The fish feels the feeder when it hits the top of the loop, darts away, and hooks itself. Line breaking strain should also be increased to at least 4 lb, and the swimfeeder itself can be attached via a short loop of elasticated power gum to increase its shock- absorbing qualities. Swimfeeders are as much a part of the modern match angler's repertoire as rods and reels, and as you become more adept at using them, try making subtle changes in the way that you fish them, such as enlarging the holes of a blockend to allow its contents to escape quicker, and cutting a feeder to shorten it and reduce the number of maggots it

63

Above: Weights can be clipped on to swimfeeders in flowing water.

Right: Aim at an object on the far bank when casting.

holds, which can be useful on hard days.

Casting has to be accurate when feeder-fishing, otherwise bait will be deposited all over your swim. Select an object on the far bank as your target and aim towards that every time. Then it's just a question of consistency of distance. Some anglers, once they are happy with their distance, slip their line under the line clip that is now included on the spools of most reels. As long as they cast so that all the line is released as far down as that behind the clip, they can then be certain that they are casting the same distance every time. However, such a practice is only recommended when fish like bream – which are unlikely to take line once they are hooked – are expected, because no line can be released beyond that behind the clip. When you are trying to outcast your neighbours, you can use a shock leader of something like 6 lb line. This is a length of line of around twice the length of the rod, tied to the main line with a blood knot at the top and running straight through to the feeder.

64

CHAPTER SIX

BAIT

....

When it comes to deciding on what bait to use in a contest, the match angler is spoilt for choice. There are maggots, pinkies, squatts (all in various colours), casters, bread in its many forms, hemp, tares, at least three types of worm, steak, luncheon meat, sweetcorn, bloodworm and jokers. The list is almost endless, and if the match angler is to enjoy his share of success he might have to take them all! That's one of the reasons why match fishing can be an expensive game if you are to do it properly. For example, let's assume that you are fishing a match on a river that is dominated by roach and chub, but where you know one shoal of bream live, and it is these fish that will probably win the match. Now roach and chub don't pose a problem. A few pints of maggots and some hemp will be fine for these. But what about those bream? If you're lucky enough to draw on the shoal, you will need some casters, perhaps some squatts, groundbait – and don't forget the worms. Your bait bill is rising dramatically. Of course, you can take a chance and not take these bream baits; and who knows, you might even catch them on maggot. However, deep down you are only too aware that maggots are not as good as casters and squatts for bream, so into your bait-bag they go. If you're fishing a match, you have to go prepared for any eventuality. It's as simple as that, even if you take a lot of your bait home again.

Top-quality maggots are a must.

Maggots

These are the most popular match-angling bait and account for more match wins than any other. They will take just about every species of coarse fish and are equally effective on a tiny canal, massive lake or a fast-flowing river. The largest maggot and the one most commonly used as hookbait is the larva of the bluebottle. Ask for 1 pt of plain maggots in your tackle shop and this is what you will get. However, once you have taken them home, there are few things that you should do to improve the quality of the bait. First, run the bait through a maggot riddle. You can make this yourself, or buy one from the tackle shop. Simply place the riddle over a bowl, pour the maggots on to it, and let them wriggle through. If you have a lot of maggots it's best to do this in small batches otherwise the weight of those on top will prevent those underneath from wriggling through. Once all the bait has been sent through the riddle, discard any dead maggots or other unwanted material left on the riddle. At this point there should be no casters at all, as your maggots should be very fresh and several days away from turning. If they're not – you can tell a fresh maggot by its large, dark feed spot – then complain, or change your tackle dealer. Let's assume that you are left with good, lively maggots plus the medium in which they were supplied. This might be sawdust, bran or, more commonly, maize meal. Your next job is to remove this and replace it with some of your own. Simply pour some of the maggots back on to the riddle and, working quickly, agitate it so that the medium falls through and you are left with the maggots on top. Pour them into another bowl. Repeat this process several times until you are left with just the maggots. Keep the riddle still for more than a second and some will work their way through. Now you can add whatever you want to keep your bait in. Maize meal is the best for maggots that are to be used as hookbait, and your tackle dealer will sell you some. It degreases them, keeps them clean and dry, and doesn't smell. Don't add too much or you might have problems finding maggots among the maize meal. Add just enough so that every maggot receives a fine coating of the stuff.

That is all you need to do with maggots if you are to leave them uncoloured. However, many anglers prefer to use bronze and red maggots for match fishing, probably out of habit, but old habits die hard, and roach and chub certainly seem to love them. Red maggots are usually 'colour-fed'. The maggot breeder adds red dye to the meat on which the growing grubs are feeding, which means that the red dye is inside the bait and will not come off on your hands. However, bronze maggots – the most popular coloured maggot of them all – are usually dyed by the tackle dealer, and if you're not careful you could end up with bronze hands.

Bronze maggots also need cleaning very well as described, and it will also pay you to change your own maize meal two or three times, the final change being on the morning of the match. As you discard each batch of maize meal, you will notice that it is orange. This is the excess dye that has not been absorbed by the maggots. Many tackle dealers now use alternatives to chrysoidine, the orange or bronze dye that was traditionally used for maggots, as several years ago it was linked with cancer. However, some still use chrysoidine, so the need for cleanliness is vital. If you want to dye your own white maggots bronze, don't use chrysoidine. Try one of the non-toxic alternatives that are available, or use turmeric. This orange powder is available from tackle shops, but you'll get it cheaper from Indian grocers as it is a ground, dried root used in Eastern cookery. You should simply keep the maggots in turmeric rather than maize meal once you get them home from the shop, replacing it with maize meal on the morning of the match. You will see that the turmeric doesn't dye the maggot very deeply, more of a light shade of orange, but usually this is enough. In fact, many good river anglers feed with turmeric maggots and fish with either a darker, shop-bought orange one or a red one on the hook. These 'target baits' often produce a bite as they offer the fish something a little different.

Maggots are used mainly as hookbait, loose feed and in a blockend swimfeeder. It's best not to add any to groundbait, or at least very few, as they tend to break the balls up too quickly as they wriggle around. Pinkies and squatts are much better for this as they are smaller. Pinkies, the larva of the greenbottle fly, are slimmer than big maggots and often used as feed in small waters, and on the hook either singly or in pairs. In fact you should always try two red pinkies for bream fishing. This combination can often produce more fish than any other. You should clean pinkies when you get them home in the same way as maggots, although you will need a riddle with smaller holes. Again these are available from your tackle shop.

Instead of maize meal, store pinkies in fine sawdust. This seems to keep them fresher, as well as enabling them to be fired further with a catapult, although still not as far as big maggots as they are much lighter. Pinkies should be high on the list of your bait requirements for matches on waters where small fish – especially roach and gudgeon – that can soon be filled up by big maggots are the target. It is fine for small fish to be filled up quickly if there is something larger to take their place, but fatal if you plan to catch these small fish every day. Obviously, homework is important here. If you know that big roach will win the match, you can start by catching with

67

Adding squatts to groundbait can be deadly for bream.

pinkies, but try to increase the feed as the match progresses, or start to add a few big maggots in with the pinkies. Any larger fish that are prepared to feed will soon home in and drive the smaller ones away. Pinkies can also be added in moderate numbers to groundbait, although they are active so don't overdo it or the balls will break up too quickly, in mid-air or well before they reach the bottom.

The match angler's third maggot is the squatt, the larva of the house fly. These strange looking maggots need different treatment from their larger cousins as they do not suffer the cold as well and are best kept in the red foundry sand in which they are supplied. Keep this sand slightly damp to the touch by using a gardener's atomiser spray filled with water. During summer matches you might find that you need to spray them every hour or so, but only lightly. Squatts are a brilliant bait for bream when added to groundbait, but they are also much used by anglers after good match catches of small fish. You might need at least 1 pt of squatts on a prolific canal or drain venue to keep a shoal of small roach happy all day, and some anglers have made a real art of amassing large weights of these small fish, following around the swim by casting a small waggler to different places or adding and taking off individual pole sections. Numerous depth changes are also required. It's hard work, but very rewarding.

To keep your bait in tip-top condition, invest in a second-hand bait fridge. You should be able to pick one up for a fiver or so fairly quickly and the fridge will soon become an invaluable aid to ensuring good-quality bait when it's operational in your garage or shed. All of your maggots should be kept in the fridge in bait- boxes with the lids off, and don't put too many maggots in a box, or those underneath might suffocate. Take great care with squatts; they are extremely delicate and soon die if they become too cold. Some anglers only put squatts in the fridge in the hottest weather. At other times they will keep for a week or so in a bait-box – lid off – on the garage floor. Many match anglers would not keep bait from one week to the next, insisting on fresh bait for every competition. However, there is nothing wrong with keeping it for a week or so, especially in the case of maggots and pinkies. You can always buy a few fresh ones for use on the hook the following week. Of course, your old hook maggots can also be used for casters.

Casters

Casters are still a relatively new bait to the match angler. Their true worth was only appreciated when somebody realised that there is a period in the life cycle of a fly when the

Above: Your casters should be crisp and fresh.

Below: A maggot-caught chub approaches the net.

chrysalis sinks. Although the sinking stage is relatively short, if the chrysalis could be used for bait during this time, it could have devastating effects. Now, of course, casters are as much a part of the match angler's armoury as maggots. Most tackle dealers sell their own casters, but you need to order them in advance. However, many match anglers who want the best bait that they can lay their hands on, produce them themselves. It's a simple process that involves buying enough maggots for turning into casters at least a week before the match when you want to use them.

You will need to buy more maggots than you want casters as usually up to a quarter of them will not turn in time. Once you have taken them home from the tackle shop, run the bait through a maggot riddle to remove any dead skins and other items, and also remove the material in which they are supplied – probably maize meal – in the same way as you clean maggots. Then add plenty of fine, damp sawdust to the bait. This dampness is important as it helps the bait keep its size and produce bigger casters. Leave the bait in a bowl with the lid off for several days, keeping the sawdust damp by spraying it every day with an atomiser. In summer, it pays to place the bowl of maggots in a fridge until about five days before you want to use them. Keep your eye on the bait, checking that nothing much happens until Tuesday, assuming that you want the bait for the following weekend. Then you should see the first of the light-coloured casters in among the maggots. Run the lot through your maggot riddle. If there are only a few casters, but plenty of dead skins, discard the lot. If there are more casters, quickly pick out and throw away the skins, but wrap the casters in a sheet of damp newspaper and place this in a polythene bag in your bait fridge. The damp newspaper prevents the casters acquiring 'fridge burns', when the part of the caster touching the side of the polythene bag turns a darker shade then the rest of it.

Keep the sawdust damp with an atomiser spray and riddle the maggots at least twice, preferably three times, a day. Add each batch of casters to the first ones you ran off, removing any dead skins as you do so. Now simply continue running the casters off regularly to produce your own perfect bait. Once you have enough to fill a bait-box, fill it to the brim and place a sheet of polythene between casters and lid to keep it airtight. If there's a gap, fill it with folded, dampened newspaper. Neglect this and the air in the box will soon turn the casters into useless floaters.

Casters are a universal bait for the match angler, working for fickle canal roach, for big chub in rivers, and for large shoals of hungry bream. Once introduced into a swim as feed, they cannot wriggle away, and when used on the hook, they tend to avoid the attentions of small, nuisance fish. It's always worth taking some with you, you never know when you might need them.

Punched bread

An increasingly popular matchman's bait, especially in winter, is punched bread. The effectiveness of this bait has come to light in recent seasons as an alternative to bloodworm and jokers, now banned on many venues up and down the country. For some reason, punched bread works when moving baits like maggots, pinkies and squatts can hardly entice a bite. Prepare a few slices from a white, medium-sliced loaf and use the rest for feed by putting the slices with the crusts cut off into a liquidiser and grinding them until you produce fine breadcrumbs. This liquidised bread makes an excellent feed for a match where you intend to fish with punched bread, but take care as it can fill the fish up quickly. With small roach, the usual punched-bread quarry, it doesn't take much to satisfy a shoal – fine if there are a lot of fish in your swim, but dangerous if bites are few and far between. Liquidised bread holds together when squeezed and can be thrown a reasonable distance with accuracy. It tends to float on the surface for a few seconds, releasing tiny particles, before sinking out of sight.

To prepare slices for use on the hook, cut the crusts off, carefully steam them over boiling water – placing each slice on a fish slice is a good idea – and flatten them with a rolling pin before placing them in individual food bags. Use one slice every hour of the contest to ensure freshness, which in turn will help the bread stay on the hook longer. Some anglers don't steam their bread for use as punch, preferring the piece to swell up in the water. Choose your bread punches carefully. The best ones are shallow and made from metal. They cut the slice neatly to produce a piece of bread that is somewhat compressed and stays on the hook well.

Match anglers intent on doing well on waters containing large numbers of small roach often start off with punched bread, as it tends to produce a very fast response. If you don't catch within 10 minutes, the chances are that you won't catch at all with the bait. However, if fish do start to come, you might be in for a great day. Catch on punched bread for five hours and you have done very well and can be pleased with your achievement. Far more likely is that you catch on the bait for the first hour or two before the fish seem to go off the bait. That should be your signal to change to another bait, usually pinkies, fished in conjunction with loose-fed pinkies or squatts, or small but regular balls of groundbait containing a few hookbait samples.

71

Perfectly cooked hempseed is a good bait at any time of the year.

Seed baits

Cooked seeds such as hemp, tares and wheat have accounted for a lot of match wins over the years, especially when big roach are the quarry, but it is a brave angler who takes seeds to a match with no other bait as a back-up. The reason for this is that, while seed baits account for hundreds of memorable catches for pleasure anglers every season, they enjoy nowhere near that amount of success in matches, probably because of the numbers of maggots being introduced by nearby anglers. However, many match anglers swear by hempseed as feed when they are fishing for roach. A combination of hemp and maggot loose feed tends to draw a larger-than-average size of roach into the swim, and you can always slip a grain of hemp on to the hook after a time. If you start to get bites and fish, you could be in for a good catch of big roach. If you get bites but only succeed in missing most of them, the fish are not taking the seeds properly, or perhaps the culprits are small fish merely plucking at the bait. Too many anglers persevere with hempseed on the hook in this situation, trying different hook sizes and shotting patterns, but it can become an obsession and before they know it the match is nearly over and valuable time has been lost. Use them with care.

Worms

The three types of worm of interest to the match angler are redworms, brandlings and lobworms. When bream are the quarry, legered redworms take some beating, usually tempting the biggest fish from a shoal. Try one large or two small redworms on the hook, tipped with pinkie or a caster. Brandlings are slightly inferior to redworms, but more easily obtained and they too can be deadly for bream. Lobworms were not considered a bait for match anglers (apart from those fishing for chub on flooded rivers) until recently, when it was discovered that several chopped up lobworms introduced into a swim could have devastating effects, especially in stillwaters such as canals and drains and especially for perch.

Usually fished in conjunction with poles, three or four chopped lobworms are introduced to the swim by means of a small cup attached close to the pole tip. A short piece of redworm is then used on the hook with the float set so that the bait hangs just off the bottom, right over the place where the lobworms have been introduced. The response can take you by surprise, transforming a poor swim into a good one in minutes. Don't add any more feed until bites tail off, and then introduce a couple more chopped lobworms. Place the whole worms inside the pole cup and chop them up with a small pair of scissors, before pushing the pole out to deposit them in the swim. You will probably need to dip the cup in the water to release its contents. Make sure that you agitate the hookbait constantly, lifting the pole so that the bait rises an inch or two and moves to one side. If there are any perch or ruffe in the vicinity, they will soon home in on the worms, but the method will account for plenty of other species as well. It can work on even very hard days and some anglers have won hundreds of pounds using this method. Bites might be few and far between on certain venues, but when this is the case the bites you get are often from good-quality fish.

Bloodworm and jokers

These two baits are usually fished in conjunction with each other, with jokers introduced as feed and bloodworm on the hook. Both are water-dwelling larvae of midge-type insects that are collected in their millions by specialist dealers who then sell them to tackle shops or individuals. Very expensive to buy, both bloodworm and jokers are banned from many matches up and down the country among claims that they catch only tiny, immature fish, ruin a fishery for pleasure anglers who cannot afford the bait, and allow almost total domination to those anglers fortunate or rich enough to take a lot of them. While not wanting to enter into the arguments for and against these baits, it is worth noting that they will entice fish when everything else fails. They are almost always fished on pole tackle, with bloodworm being used on tiny size 24 or 26 hooks. Surprisingly, such small hooks are not really necessary, such is the liking of the fish for the bait, and some anglers use fine-wire size 18s for single bloodworm or even jokers.

However, jokers are usually employed as feed, fed either in balls of groundbait or introduced by means of a pole cup in small doses, held together by special clay. There is little scope for a Continental-style bombardment of big balls of groundbait in British match fishing. Usually packed with jokers, this generous introduction of bait at the start of a contest is designed to get large numbers of fish into the swim quickly because Continental matches are only of three-hour duration. It is unlikely that such a bombardment would keep the fish occupied for longer than that, and 'top-ups' rarely work. As British matches usually last five hours, it is better to build up a swim slowly, working towards a productive second half of the contest.

73

Other baits

There are numerous other baits that the match angler should consider, according to the venue he is fishing. Sweetcorn makes a good standby for tench and carp, and with increasing numbers of specialist match fisheries containing these species it is always worth keeping a can or two of this as a standby. Luncheon meat is also good for carp and chub, while beef steak has enjoyed considerable success on rivers such as the Trent in recent seasons where chub are the quarry. In fact, this bait is worth trying on any river where the fish seem to be turning away from maggots and casters. Simply use a small piece of steak (little larger than a maggot) on the hook, either floatfished or legered, and feed the swim with balls of minced beef bound together with maize meal or groundbait. The hookbait needs changing regularly as it appears that it is the blood and juices from the meat that are the attractors.

Groundbait

Walk into any tackle shop and you will be amazed at the array of groundbait on the shelves. Not so long ago, British anglers had to make do with two basic types – white and brown. White was used for deep water and brown for shallow. How times have changed! Now dozens of different types of groundbait are available, mostly made abroad and imported by British-based distributors. It is a confusing business for beginners and experts alike, but the best advice is to keep things simple. Try a couple of well-established groundbaits and see how you get on with them.

Although there is a wide variety to choose from, some groundbaits stand head and shoulders above the rest in terms of sales. This is no accident. They sell because they are good. Continental groundbaits do much more than merely feed the fish, and groundbaiting is now a highly specialised art, practised in several different ways from regular introductions of tiny, thumb-nail sized pieces to larger balls of groundbait. Of course, match anglers have led the way here because of the necessity of having an extra edge, and there are now groundbaits designed not only for different species, but for different waters as well.

The decision whether or not to use groundbait in a competition should not be taken lightly, for there's no doubt about it, groundbait can be the kiss of death on many days. Just as often, fish can be slow to respond to loose feed, but a little groundbait can change all that. Match-fishing trends often determine whether fish like groundbait. For example, it has become the matchman's tradition to loose-feed bronze

74

maggots for catches of good-quality roach – and sometimes hempseed as well. Good catches of roach have been taken by anglers doing this, so that's what the rest do. Similarly, it has become the norm now to introduce three or four balls of groundbait at the start of a match where you think you might catch bream. These balls are designed to attract and hold a shoal of bream in your swim, even if you do not begin by fishing for them. Many good bream match anglers like to give a bream swim an hour or two until the fish are feeding confidently before trying to catch them. However, sometimes it is the match angler who is prepared to go against the norm who enjoys sudden success, and the angler who tries groundbaiting for roach on a river, or throwing in two bowlfuls of groundbait for bream, might be pleasantly surprised and enjoy a good run, until everyone else finds out what he is doing.

Choice of which Continental-type groundbait to use is very much a personal thing, depending on how you want the groundbait to react in the water. If you are fishing for bottom-feeding fish on a deep, flowing river, for example, you will need groundbait that will fall quickly through the water once it has been moulded into balls, and not drift gently down into the next angler's swim. This groundbait is likely to contain quite large particles and be fairly sticky once mixed. On shallower waters when you want to produce a cloud effect to attract fish, a finer groundbait is required. Mix it by adding only a minimum of water so that it only just holds together when squeezed and disperses immediately on hitting the surface, sending its attractive cloud through the surface layers and falling slowly to the bottom. There are many groundbaits in between these two. Some are designed for long-range bream fishing, able to be thrown a long way by catapult but dispersing quickly if required in shallow water. Others can carry a lot of loose offerings without the balls breaking up in mid air, while others still have many 'active' particles that move up and down in the water. Texture, flavour and activity are all important. Hit upon the right combination of all three and you're on to a winner.

Of course, plain brown or white breadcrumbs also have their place, and the best 'plain' groundbait of all is slicer crumb – the particles created by the machine in the bakery that slices up a loaf. This groundbait has no foreign bodies and groundbait distributors grind it down to varying degrees of coarseness before selling it as either brown or white crumb. Brown crumb tends to be lighter than white and good for fish feeding near the surface or in shallow water, while white crumb is heavy and can be used to add weight to continental groundbait to allow it to be fired a long way by catapult, or fall quickly through the water.

Groundbait comes in many colours and textures.

Correct groundbait mixing is a vital part of the match angler's repertoire, and the best groundbait in the world will be useless unless it is mixed in the right way. Some matchmen even go to the trouble of mixing their groundbait the night before a match if they have done their homework and know what sort of groundbait they will need. Even if you intend to mix it on the waterside, make sure you do so at least half an hour before the start of the match as it absorbs a lot of water. Put the dry groundbait into a round bowl and add water in small consignments from a sponge or bait-box, mixing the groundbait well with one hand as you do so. Agitate the groundbait between your fingers until you have got rid of most of the lumps and you can squeeze it into balls. Now leave it alone for 10 minutes, when it should feel much drier. If you think that more water should be added, repeat the process until you are happy with the mix. Now pass the lot through a maggot riddle into another bowl and you have the perfect groundbait.

CHAPTER SEVEN

RIVERS

Now that you have a good knowledge of what match fishing is all about, it is time to start looking at venues. As mentioned earlier, many match anglers begin their competitive careers by concentrating their attentions on one or two venues. Others prefer to branch out and fish a variety of different places in the hope of improving their overall skills. Whichever you choose, you will have the same ultimate goal: to beat those anglers pegged either side of you. If you beat them, and they beat their neighbours on the other side, and so on along the bank, you will win. Nothing could be simpler, or could it? Here lies the fundamental difference between match fishing and 'pleasure' fishing. When you're by yourself, you only have one thing to beat - the fish. In a match, you're fishing against other anglers as well. Too many forget this and are oblivious to what's going on close by. In the following examples, you are faced with five typical river situations. You have done your homework and know roughly what to expect, but you will still have to go all out to win the match.

It is vitally important for the match-man to feed his swim regularly.

In all of them, it is assumed that you are fishing as an individual, either to win the match or, if that is not possible, to win your section.

Match one

Venue - slow river.
Time of year - autumn, warm.
Target species - roach.
Wind - slight.

It's a lovely day, perfect for a suntan, but you're not interested in that. You have to try to catch fish when, at this time of year, most of them would not be interested in feeding. Roach are your quarry, but it's unlikely that anybody will catch a big weight. On days like this, it's probable that 5 lb could get you

Don't neglect the surface layers of the water.

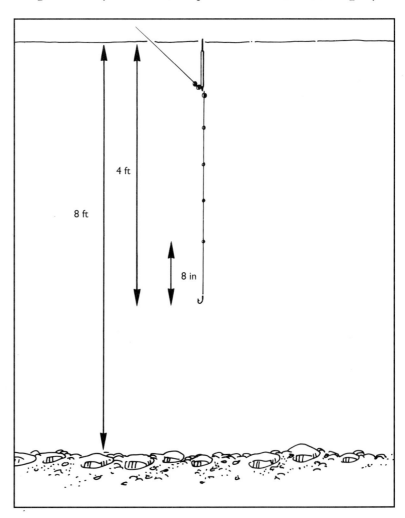

8 ft

4 ft

8 in

78

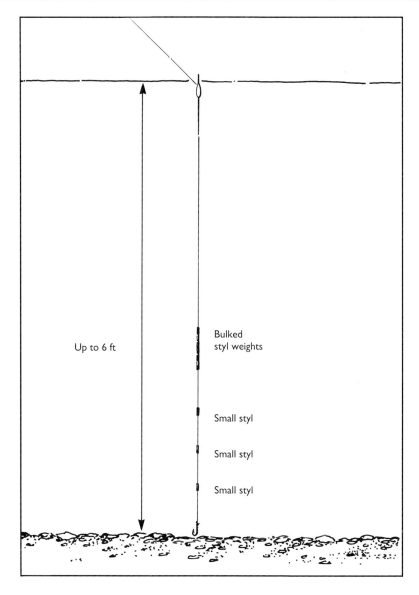

A typical summer river rig – ideal in depths up to 6 ft.

Up to 6 ft

Bulked styl weights

Small styl

Small styl

Small styl

in the frame, unless everything goes extremely well or the fish really decide to have a go. Even if you are prepared for everything, you will still have your work cut out and you will need to fish your heart out to win, or even to make the frame. If you know the river at all, you will also have some idea of what to set up.

On most river venues your tackle will be limited to waggler and pole, with the waggler fishing out in the middle or beyond, and the pole as something to try closer in. That means a 13 ft hollow-tipped rod with soft, tip-to-middle action, and a long pole fitted with No. 4 elastic. This strength will be perfect for those 3 oz and 4 oz roach that make up most of the match weights at this time of year. Use line of 2 lb

79

**Rivers in summer can
be difficult.**

breaking strain on an open-face reel, with a three AAA
waggler that is big enough to cast across without exerting too
much force into the cast. Summer roach are likely to feed not
only on the bottom, but well off it as well. Depending on the
depth, they will sometimes venture right up to a couple of
feet below the surface in the warmest weather, so the shotting
between float and hook should be light. Aim for one No. 8 for
every 18 in of depth, and space the individual weights equally
between float and hook.

Here, maggot will be the only bait that you should consider, although hempseed can be loose-fed depending on the mood of the fish and, of course, on what is happening around you. In fact, it is hempseed that could well come into its own on your close-in line for the pole, because the chances are that the roach in your swim will be prepared to eat hempseed. Despite many opinions to the contrary, hempseed does work in matches, not all matches admittedly, but the fact is that if you do start to catch with hempseed on the hook, those anglers around you can usually pack up and go home. It seems to hold some sort of magnetic attraction to roach, and they're usually bigger than those you catch on maggot.

Depending on the depth, use a pole float taking between ½ g and 1 g, and shot it with an olivette and three styl weights below. Don't use round split shot when hemp fishing. Most anglers find that using split shot gives rise to false bites when the fish take the shot, mistaking it for hempseed. Plumb carefully, and start with the bait 1 in off the bottom.

Two pints of maggots and the same of hempseed should be ample for today's match, and expect to take some home again. When the contest starts, watch how the anglers around you begin. See who starts on the rod and reel, and who starts on the pole. In most situations you would do better to begin on the pole, while feeding both pole and waggler lines. If you start on the waggler, you will bring in any fish that you catch right through your pole swim, making it a waste of time. Begin on the pole, and you can make the most of both swims, the close-in one early on, and the further one later in the match if the pole line dries up.

Loose-feed regularly in both areas, mainly with maggots on the waggler line and hempseed on the pole line, but on the latter begin with a maggot on the hook. Hemp rarely works immediately, but you will soon know whether the bait is worth a try if you start to catch reasonable-sized roach. If you do, slide a grain of hempseed on the same hook and see what happens. You will have been using a size 20 or 22 for maggot, but an 18 is better for hempseed, so if you do start to get bites, change.

Some anglers who own two pole-top kits will have taken the trouble to set up two pole rigs, one for maggot with a size 22 hook, and one, perhaps slightly lighter rig, with a size 18 for hempseed. Should hempseed work, stop feeding maggots completely and concentrate on hempseed only on the pole line, but still continue to feed the waggler line. Half a dozen grains every five minutes should be enough to keep the shoal happy, and if you do everything correctly there is no reason why you should not continue catching all day. Of course, if anglers around you are catching using wagglers, you would be a fool not to try it occasionally. Not only will it catch you a few fish, it will also give your close-in line a rest, important if you are to keep your swim active for the full five hours.

Match two

Venue - moderate-paced river.
Time of year - winter.
Target species - roach and chub.
Wind - moderate downstream.

For this imaginary match situation, a new species comes into the equation. You know there are chub in the area, and the chances are that you will need at least a couple of these fish if you are to win any money. However, you should be equally aware that you must not destroy any chances you have of amassing a good catch of roach. The secret is in the feeding. The only bait worth taking with you is maggots, 4 pt of them. Leave everything else at home – it will only confuse you. Hempseed is unlikely to be effective at this time of year as the water temperature starts to fall, and anyway is not really a bait worth considering if you are trying to catch a chub or two.

You should plan three lines of attack, and expect to use them all at some time during the day. The waggler is likely to be your main catching method here. If the river is of only moderate width, say 30 yd or less, it is certainly worth checking out the far side. Are there any overhanging trees opposite. If there are, your chances of catching chub are good, especially if 'your' tree is one of only a few along the stretch, so concentrate your waggler line there. However, if the far bank is quite featureless, pick a comfortable casting area, checking the depth by pushing the float up the line, casting out and repeating the process until eventually the float is pulled under as the hook becomes caught up on the bottom. Make sure that you use a waggler whose weight-carrying capacity allows you to reach your desired casting spot with ease, remembering that the awkward downstream wind might increase as the contest progresses. Make several trial casts to discover where the float enjoys an unhindered passage through the swim. If the bottom is fairly clean, the chances are that the fish will be in that vicinity.

Your second line of attack should be the stick float. Even in these potentially awkward conditions for a top-and-bottom float, it is worth setting up a stick float with heavy stem made from lignum wood or even plastic. These stems will allow you to fish the float reasonably comfortably, and you should be able to reap the benefits offered by this method. If the

82

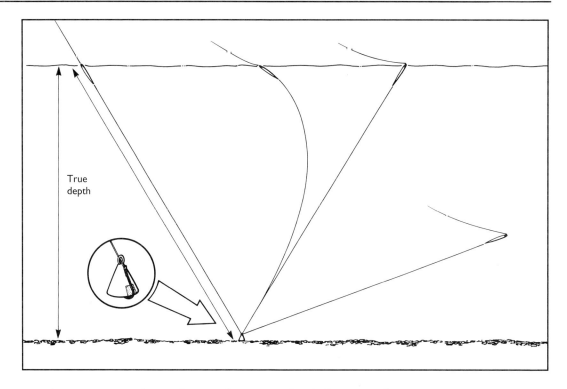

True
depth

wind is strong, try the technique known as backshotting. This involves fixing one, or in extreme conditions, two No. 8 shot between 6 in and 1 ft above the float to sink the last part of your line below the surface. It is this part of your line that often ruins a stick float's presentation in a downstream wind.

The third rod you should set up is a link leger. This is not the desperate method some anglers would have you believe. All you need are one or two 8 oz fish later on in the competition and you will be elevated from the ranks of the also rans to right up there among the winners. Use a soft quivertip rod with a simple paternoster rig, and SSG shot instead of a single leger weight. Vary the number of weights on the link according to where you are casting. You need just enough to make the weight hold bottom. This method can work at all times during a match on this type of venue, especially when you cast towards the bottom end of your swim. Try it on both waggler and stick float lines.

Mindful that chub are your quarry as well as roach, you'd be better off here starting on the waggler, feeding around 30 maggots every cast and fishing with the bait just trundling along the bottom. Feed the close-in stick float line as well, but with only around a dozen maggots every few minutes. Throw these in slightly downstream of where you are fishing. The idea of this is to make a feeding area some way down your swim so that any fish you catch on the waggler don't scare those feeding on the close-in line, and so that you can cast

Plumb the depth carefully to obtain a true reading.

83

your stick float some way down your swim – for better control in the downstream wind – and not miss any fish because you're fishing downstream of them. Again, watch what's happening around you. If you see no chub being caught, be happy with what you are doing as long as you're catching. However, if chub are being caught, you will have to try different methods to keep in touch. There are two main things to try in this situation.

The first is to try fishing at different depths. Often chub will feed up in the water, intercepting the bait before the more timid roach get to it. Try up to just 3 ft under the surface, or even shallower if the water's only 5 ft deep in the first place.

The other trick is to increase the feed suddenly. This, in truth, is something of a last resort and best done only in the last hour when all seems lost. Of course, perhaps you are happy with your section-winning roach catch even though you have heard that someone elsewhere has caught some chub. However, if you want to win, try this sudden increase in feed. It can have surprising results.

Stick and link leger? These are your two back-up roach methods. The chances are that they won't produce too many fish, but those fish that they do catch are likely to be of good quality.

Top match-man Dave Harrell is a master of the stick float.

Match three

Barbel like this beauty can ensure victory on many rivers.

Venue - fast river.
Time of year - summer.
Target species - barbel and chub.
Wind - upstream.

It looks like you could be in for a good day. The water is warm, the fish are feeding and with chub and barbel the quarry, there is every chance of taking a big catch. Summer bait requirements for a match on this venue will be considerable, and you should be thinking about using as much as 1 gal in a five-hour contest. Split this into 4 pt of hemp and 4 pt of casters and the expense is slightly reduced. No maggots? Take a few bronze and red ones for hookbait, but the problem with this sort of venue in summer is often that it seems to be teeming with minnows that make mincemeat out of maggots before anything larger can get a look in. Once the big fish do arrive, the minnows will disappear, but by feeding large amounts of hemp and casters you should avoid them altogether.

Two methods are likely to be required, swimfeeder and waggler. The feeder should be of the blockend variety, rigged up on a short loop and fished with a fairly stout quivertip rod. If the barbel do move in, you will soon discover their fighting

85

Stop chub jumping out of your keepnet by placing your landing net over its mouth.

qualities, so you will need the end tackle to be able to subdue them. Line of 4 lb breaking strain, hooklength of 3 lb and size 18 or 16 forged hook are the order of the day. Make sure the feeder has enough weight on the side for it to hold bottom. In some swims that might mean as much as 3 oz. You will need to carry some special clip-on lead strips for the job.

Floatfishing can be highly rewarding as well as enjoyable in this sort of swim, which usually responds best to a short, dumpy waggler made from peacock quill and taking enough weight to cast easily to your fishing spot. Depth is likely to be little more than 5 ft so you will need only three or four No. 8 shot between float and hook. Again, thicker line is required than you would usually use for floatfishing, together with bigger hooks and stronger hooklengths. Go for something like a 3 lb main line, size 18 or 16 hook and 2 lb hooklength. A float rod with a bit of power behind it will also be preferable, as will an open-face reel because closed-face reels are not really strong enough for the job.

The chances are that all the anglers around you are equally aware of the venue's potential for chub and barbel, but it's unlikely that many will have set up a float rod. This is where you can score. By floatfishing, especially early on in the contest, you can catch fish that have not yet fully congregated on your loose feed, you won't scare these still-uncertain fish by splashing a swimfeeder down on top of them, and you'll still have time to loose-feed a lot of bait. Starting on the float with two red maggots, feed two or three big catapult pouchfuls of your caster and hempseed combination every cast. Make sure your line floats perfectly – treat it beforehand with line floatant spray – and simply cast, leave the bale arm open on the reel, and let the flow do the rest. Don't worry too much if you haven't caught anything after 45 minutes. Just keep that feed going and eventually the fish should arrive. When they do, you should be ready for them.

Chub pose few problems, apart from an awkward habit of diving into close-in weed-beds just when you think that you have them beaten. The trick is to bring them to the top a rod-length or two out into the river – not too far out though, or they might be splashing about right over the shoal which is fatal in shallow water. Barbel are a different proposition altogether, charging off on seemingly unstoppable runs when you first hit them and fighting every inch of the way to the net. With strong tackle you should land them, but don't try to bring them to the net before they are ready – that's a recipe for disaster.

Eventually, the time will come when the fish are feeding confidently enough for the feeder to be used. Cast out and hold the rod high so that the tip is well away from the water. Watch for bites shown both when the tip bounces forwards and when it drops back. By casting regularly with a feederful of casters and hempseed, you will ensure a steady supply of loose feed to the swim. In fact, at this point you should stop loose-feeding by catapult altogether, as the aim now is to congregate the fish in a small area around your hookbait. Ironically, the feeder will also be your best method if bites are very hard to come by. A baited hook left in the same place for a long time is sometimes the only way to tempt fish that are unwilling to feed. They seem to take the bait out of sheer frustration. It is also self-regulating – the more you catch, the more you feed, and the less you cast, the less you feed.

Match four

Venue - slow river.
Time of year - summer.
Target species - bream.
Wind - strong downstream.

Conditions on the day go a long way to determining your approach to any match, and this one is a typical example. On the vast majority of occasions, bream, today's target species, will only take a still or very slowly moving bait. In a strong downstream wind, you would find it impossible to make a floatfished bait behave in this way apart from using impractical and inefficient techniques such as float legering. So this is really a one- method match, and that method is legering. As it's windy a swingtip would also be difficult to

87

Groundbait is a must for bream.

use properly, so again the decision has been made for you. The only rod that you should consider is the quivertip variety.

Before choosing your tip, assess the conditions. You want a quivertip that is sensitive, that doesn't get blown around by the wind, and that doesn't get pulled round too much by the surface tow caused by the wind. So choose the tip you think is right, but be prepared to change it if you have to. This should be fished with an open-face reel, 2 lb line, 1½ lb hooklength and a size 20 or 18 microbarbed hook. An open-end swimfeeder will be the best method. Choose a medium-sized one and use it on a 6 in link with a 4 ft tail. Three rod-rests are used to keep the rod stable with one 3 ft from the rod tip, one midway along, and one by your upper leg. A target board might also come in useful as a background against which to spot bites. Even big bream are sometimes shy feeders, moving the tip perhaps 1 in or less.

You might notice other anglers around you setting up wagglers for roach, and perhaps a long pole for eels. By all means do so as well, but if you are fishing to win the match you know that you will need bream. You might only need one to win your section – one 5 lb bream is the equivalent of a lot of 2 oz roach or eels! You'll also need groundbait for these bream. Perhaps you have confidence in plain breadcrumbs, but you would be wise to add a little extra flavouring or texture in the form of Continental groundbait or

A typical small-fish match-winning bag for Kim Milsom.

89

additive. Take time mixing the groundbait and make sure it is ready a good 10 minutes before the start. Bait requirements for a bream match such as this will usually include casters and squatts – 1 pt or two of each should be enough – and assorted hookbaits such as maggots, pinkies, perhaps a slice or two of bread and, most important, worms. Decide where you're going to cast and make a mental note of an object on the far bank to aim at. You'll probably do best fishing well over half way across the river as well, if only to avoid those around you loose-feeding maggots along the middle. The last thing that you want is a shoal of roach or eels moving in on your bream feed.

Once the match starts, see whether other anglers introduce groundbait around you. If they do, try to catapult yours somewhere different, preferably further out. Add a couple of good handfuls of casters and squatts to your mixed groundbait and fire in three or four balls the size of tennis balls. Use a Whopper Dropper type of catapult for this, and mould the balls with wet hands to form a skin and prevent them breaking up in mid-air. Try to be as accurate as possible, but don't worry too much if the balls spread out a little. Bream are grazers and a shoal will cover quite a wide area while feeding. Now bait your hook with a red maggot, two pinkies, caster and maggot, worm and caster or whatever. Quickly fill the feeder, making sure that you include plenty of 'meat' with the groundbait, and cast to the right spot.

Now it's very much a waiting game, remembering to add a few squatts and casters to your groundbait before filling your feeder each time. Don't add them all at once or the casters will soon become dark, useless floaters and the squatts will all wriggle to the bottom of the bowl. If bites are not forthcoming, there are several things to try. Move the bait 1 ft or so along the bottom by pulling your rod back, winding in a little to tighten up, and replacing it on the rests. Experiment with hookbaits, perhaps even trying breadflake on a larger hook if eels are a problem. Add an occasional extra ball of groundbait. It might not be until the last hour that you start to catch – if you've managed to stick it out that long while others around you have been catching a few roach and eels. However, you might need only four bream to win. In a team match, you have to catch your 'points' fish, but no one will criticise you for fishing for bream for the full duration of an individual contest, even if you end up catching none.

Match five.

Venue - river.
Time of year - winter, moderate

Target species - small roach.
Wind - slight.

Here we have a match where speed is of vital importance. The fish are small but there are lots of them and a reasonable weight is a possibility. However, most anglers will know the score so you must make sure that you have everything in your favour. You must persuade the fish to congregate in a tight area, and for this reason you should seriously consider using groundbait – small, hard balls that sink quickly to the bottom but break up and disperse once there. Add a few pinkies to this. Not too many, but enough to give the fish a sample of your hookbait. Hard balls of groundbait should ensure that the fish stay close to the bottom. You shouldn't need to loose-feed at all as this might confuse the fish and draw them up in the water, resulting in missed bites. With the fish on the bottom, and fairly close in, you will be able to catch them quickly all day, and there is no faster method for this than the whip.

On rivers, a whip of 5 m or 6 m will usually be adequate, although some anglers set up several of different lengths so that they can follow the fish out if they have to. Just as good are whips that have an add-on, take-apart section. If the fish do move out, you can add on a section every time and unship when you land a fish, or add on a section and tie on an extra metre or so of line so that you are still fishing to-hand. Your pole float should be of the shoulder-up variety. Use one large enough to take a weight that will sink the bait quickly down to the bottom. This means using a bunch of shot or an olivette with perhaps one No. 8 shot below it. The bulk should be around three-quarters of the way from float to hook.

Make sure that everything is placed within easy reach so that you don't have to move during the match. Have plenty of hooks ready tied and at least two spare pole rigs in case a disaster, such as a bag tangle, occurs. Don't waste time, either. Fish move around constantly, even if your feeding is accurate. A few runs without a bite should see you trying something different to keep in touch with them. Perhaps a pike has moved into your swim and the fish have drifted down a little. Wherever they are, you must find them quickly and, feeding in the same place all the time, draw them back up to your main catching spot. Drop your rig in underarm; don't swing it overarm as your bait will take longer to settle. And try to feed so that the fish are right at the top of the swim. You will catch them faster that way. Standing up might help as well. Speed is of the essence here, and the greater time your tackle spends in the water, the greater weight of fish you will catch. The angler who wins a 'race' like this can be proud of his achievement, and exhausted as well!

CHAPTER EIGHT

STILLWATERS

••

**Opposite: Many
stillwaters are packed
with small carp.**

Match fishing on stillwaters presents several problems that are
rarely encountered by anglers tackling flowing waters. For a
start, faced with a large expanse of open water, how do you
know where you should cast? Finding the depth and make-up
of the bottom are very important. Then there are problems
concerned with the direction of the cast. Many arguments
have ensued between neighbouring match anglers who
appeared to be casting into the same spot, probably because
one of them was sitting at a slightly different angle to the
other. Vicious undertow created by the wind can also make
life difficult, and sometimes shallow margins necessitate
wading a long way out (if the rules allow) to fish effectively
and to ensure that your keepnet is covered by enough water
to keep the fish inside happy. Catching fish can also be hard
work! Nevertheless, match fishing on stillwaters is increasingly popular, because quite often it offers more reliable
and consistent sport than other venues, especially rivers,
many of which seem to be in decline.

Well-managed, well-stocked lakes have great fish-catching
potential, especially if they contain several different species
that can be relied upon to feed at different times of the year.
Venues such as these make excellent places for the annual
club outing. Reports filter through of big catches that have
been taken from the lake in previous weeks and often the
excitement is justified, with winning weights sometimes in
excess of 50 lb. Dozens of lakes up and down the country
have been stocked with carp weighing from a few ounces to
10 lb or even more. Voracious feeders in all but the coldest
conditions, carp can provide great sport for club and open
match angler alike. When they become too big for
conventional match tackle, fishery owners often net them out,
sell them off, and replace them with a healthy stock of smaller
carp, repeating the process when these fish become too large.
It is a procedure that works, and now some match anglers fish
these carp lakes exclusively, perfecting weird and wonderful
techniques to outwit this canny fish.

Of course, there are older, more natural lakes that can be
enjoyed by the matchman and these present a very different
challenge. Here you will often have to make a decision as to
what species you are going to fish for. Will the match be won

with a weight of bream and tench, or is it too cold for them? Is it worth fishing for one or two of the big, wily carp that are known to inhabit the lake, or would you be better off going all out for the abundance of small roach that you know live close to the bank? Match fishing is all about making the right decisions, and that rule applies just as much on lakes as it does on rivers, canals and other waters. Now let's take a look at a few typical examples of matches on lakes, and see the different ways in which you should approach the different types of stillwater that you might encounter.

Match one

Venue - shallow lake.
Time of year - summer.
Target species - bream and tench.
Wind - warm, blowing from right to left.

Many large, shallow lakes are used as match venues. Unless they have been stocked with large numbers of small carp specifically for match fishing, the chances are that native bream and tench will dominate the contests. There's also likely to be a big population of roach and smaller, skimmer bream. These fish often make up section-winning bags, but only rarely will there be enough of them to produce the outright winning weight. It all depends on what you are going for. If you have done your homework and know that the peg that you have drawn gives you no chance of individual glory, by all means try to win your section with these smaller fish. However, if your peg, or the area in which you have drawn, has a proven track record of producing matchwinning bags, you might as well 'go for it' and fish for big ones. That warm wind will almost certainly stir them into feeding, but you must still ensure that you do everything right if you are to be successful.

Groundbait is important here. Make sure that you mix up the right sort. In shallow water up to about 6 ft deep, you want something that can be fired a long way by catapult, but that will break up once it has landed on the surface. It's also worth using a different mix for the swimfeeder – today's number one method for a win. For the feeder, use a dryer groundbait. It can be the same type, but with less water added, so that it holds together when squeezed inside the feeder, but only just. It will explode from the feeder when it hits the water, depositing your added loose offerings and falling through in an attractive cloud. Two groundbait bowls are required, one for the groundbait that you intend to introduce by catapult, and one for your feeder groundbait.

As for the hookbait, all the usual baits will do, such as maggots, especially red ones, worms and casters, but it's definitely worth taking some bread and sweetcorn as well. The trouble with some prolific fisheries is that small baits such as maggots and casters tend to be picked up by small fish before the big ones get a look in. You might be perfectly happy catching these smaller fish – and depending upon what else is happening in the contest, you might be wise to do so – but if you really are after the big ones, try bread or sweetcorn. Bites will be nowhere near as frequent, but when you get one, the chances are that it will be from a bigger fish. Of course, keep trying smaller baits as well to see whether the small fish have finally drifted away, leaving the big ones dominant (big fish will often take small baits when there are no small fish to get there first).

Watch out for line bites. A line bite is exactly what it suggests, an indication for all the world like a bite that is caused when a fish swims into your line. They can be a real problem, especially in shallow water, but at least it means that there are some fish out in front of you. The problem is in differentiating between a line bite and a proper bite. Always strike at the first bite of the day as no one can categorically say that your first bite was a line bite, even if it appears to be so. If it was a line bite, you will strike into nothing, the bait will be untouched, and there might even be some slime on your line some way above the hook. If it was a true bite, you will also soon know about it, with a fish in the net!

Generally speaking, line bites tend to be quick, sharp pulls on the tip, sometimes holding the quivertip out or the swingtip up for several seconds, sometimes letting it drop back again quickly. True bites tend to be steadier pulls, often preceded by a twitch or two on the tip, or a very small movement. Don't think that tiny movements are always caused by shy fish. If a fish picks up a bait and starts to eat it confidently, it may not move very far. Consequently the indication on the tip will be slight. In these situations a target board is essential. However, if the tip pulls round fast and keeps going, the fish has taken the bait, felt something suspicious and charged off, possibly scaring the other members of the shoal. Try to get the fish feeding confidently before plundering the shoal.

Match two

Venue - large lake.
Time of year - summer.
Target species - small roach, skimmer bream, rudd and perch.
Wind - in your face.

A large lake bream comes to the net.

This could be the same lake as the one described above, but in this contest small fish are the quarry and speed will be important. Ideally you will be able to catch them close to the bank, so you can fish to-hand with a whip, but you would be wise to set up waggler and pole tackle as well. In fact, with the wind blowing in your face, a top-and-bottom float fished on a whip might prove ineffective as the wind will blow it towards you. If you are getting bites very quickly, this might not matter because you will be catching fish before the wind has had time to affect the float. If bites are taking a few minutes to come,however, you might have to take action to prevent it happening.

One way is to use a bigger float taking more weight, which you fix near to the hook where the wind is having less effect on the tackle. In fact, the bottom layers of the water might well be moving in the opposite direction, away from you, as

Small floats like these are perfect for canals.

the surface layers hit the bank and push back out again underneath.

Although a bigger float sometimes works in these conditions, you would probably be better off dispensing with a top-and-bottom float altogether and using a small waggler instead. This type of float will be easy to flick out over your head against a facing wind with a whip, and after it has hit the water you should sink the line between whip tip and float by dipping the 1 ft or so of the whip under the surface and pulling sharply towards you.

In this head wind, a pole with a short line would also come in helpful as it will allow you to fish at the required distance with a light and sensitive top-and-bottom float without it drifting too close to you. You can also add a section should the fish drift further out into the lake. Set up a small waggler as well, just in case the fish have a habit of wandering around the swim still further. With a waggler, you can follow them.

As for feeding in a swim such as this one and for small fish, they will need a regular supply. Groundbait is likely to be successful. Depending on the strength of the wind, mix it very dry or very wet. A very dry mix will break up immediately on impact with the surface, but cannot be thrown with any great accuracy, whereas a very wet, sloppy mix can be thrown accurately as it is heavier, but it sinks down to the bottom

97

Small wagglers are good in windy conditions.

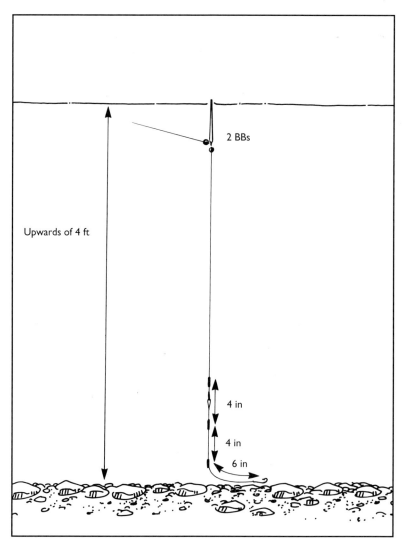

2 BBs

Upwards of 4 ft

4 in

4 in

6 in

before dispersing. How the fish are feeding should also determine the type of mix that you use – dry if they're taking on the drop, as the bait falls, or wet for fish feeding on or close to the bottom.

Match three

Venue - shallow, highly coloured lake.
Time of year - autumn.
Target species - carp up to 5 lb.
Wind - none.

Match fishing for carp can be great fun, and many match anglers are turning to shallow, well-stocked, man-made lakes because these can normally be relied upon to produce some fish. It is often said that well-managed carp lakes are the match fisheries of the future. Certainly some huge winning catches have been taken from many of the hundreds of carp match fisheries up and down the country, and they offer an exciting prospect for both club and open match anglers. Carp are ravenous feeders, rooting around on the bottom and creating a mass of suspended particles in the water, which means most good carp match fisheries are always highly coloured. This is one of the reasons why a lot of bait is often required, but before you fish your match on a carp lake, you must find out the rules of the fishery.

Many owners impose bans or restrictions on certain baits, for example hempseed and groundbait. Some even provide their own keepnets to eliminate any chance of disease from other fisheries being carried by anglers' nets, killing their valuable stock. Find out what rules and regulations you have to follow before fishing. However, don't let them worry you as the only bait that you will usually need is maggots – lots of them. Take as many as you can afford, or as many as the rules of the fishery allow. Some impose restrictions on this as well.

The waggler reigns supreme on most match carp fisheries, and if you have features in your swim, fish towards them. Carp are just like many other coarse fish species and spend much of their time around features such as overhanging trees and bushes, weed-beds, reeds, lilies and islands. If the swim you have drawn contains one or more of these, there is every chance that you will catch carp very soon. Feed up any likely-looking areas and expect to catch from more than one, taking a few fish from the first before giving it a rest and moving over to another. As the match progresses, you will probably find that one area becomes more productive than the others and you can concentrate on it during the later stages. However, if you have drawn a featureless swim, you will probably need to feed for a time to draw the carp into the area from outside.

Regular, almost constant feeding is required when you're fishing a carp lake. On a warm summer's day, that might mean 50 or more maggots for feeding every few minutes. Cold weather will demand much less feed, but still as regular. Wagglers should be of the straight variety – clear plastic ones are good for carp – and shotted with very little, if any, weight between float and hook. The reason for this is that very often carp will come right up to the surface when you're feeding constantly. You can catch a lot of fish on the drop, and by fishing shallow.

One problem that you might encounter when carp fishing is that of line bites. The fish get into such a feeding frenzy that they charge around the swim bumping into your line and

99

producing false bites. Many top carp matchmen rarely watch their float in these circumstances, but fish by placing their rod on a rest to one side, with the butt on their knee. The rod tip is used rather like a quivertip and both hands are free to feed maggots constantly by catapult. They cast out, place the rod on the rest, and feed regularly while watching the rod tip, or occasionally the float, and twitching the bait frequently by making a turn or two on the reel handle. When the tip flies round, you know that a fish has taken the bait. Vary the hookbait from single to double maggots – reds and white are best – and try floating maggots as well. To make maggots float, separate a few from the main batch and place them in a bait-box. Add just enough water to cover them and in a few minutes they will float. Two floating maggots or one floater and a sinker can make excellent alternative baits for carp.

Polefishing for carp can also be productive, but you'll need to change the elastic that you used so successfully for small roach on your local canal! Thread at least No. 6 strength through the top two sections of your pole so that it is fairly tight, and have other sections close by to add on if you have to. It is a method that can work very well when employed for fishing close to the bank, especially during the later stages of a match when the fish will have returned to feed after the initial disturbance caused by your arrival. A steady trickle of half-a-dozen maggots flicked close in will usually bring them back, especially if there is some cover close by. Use small, canal 'dibber' floats shotted lightly and be prepared for some frenetic sport if the carp do return.

Carp fishing in winter matches sometimes requires a different approach, not only in the amount that you feed, but also in the methods you employ. On really cold days when

Opposite: Small carp like this can make up match catches in excess of 100 lb.

Eels can be great fun on the pole.

you know that bites will be few and far between, it can pay to use a small blockend swimfeeder carrying maggots. Cast it accurately to the same spot every time – further out into the lake than anyone else, if possible – and eventually some carp should start to feed. Don't expect many bites, but you might need only three or four fish to win the match.

Match four

Venue - lake, very slow-moving river, or drain.
Time of year - summer.
Target species - eels.
Wind - none.

An increasing number of matches are being won in summer by anglers catching eels. Not so long ago, eels were regarded as little better than vermin by anglers, and they were banned in many contests, but all that has changed now and anybody who fishes in places where they can be found must learn how to catch them. Big catches are possible as well. On average, river eels go four to every pound of weight, but on lakes and drains, you might only need three or even two. You don't need many for 10 lb, and that will certainly win a lot of contests during summer. When match anglers first realised the potential of eels as a match-winning species, they were relatively easy to catch. After all, for years anglers had been trying not to catch them, so they were not suspicious. However, as time went by, eels become more wary of anglers' baits. Anglers have fine-tuned their methods now and eel fishing has become a skill that some anglers have mastered to the point of leaving others struggling to catch up.

Undoubtedly the best method for catching eels in matches is with a pole, fitted with fairly strong elastic – No. 6 – through the top two sections. Depending on the depth and wind conditions, your float should be of the 'shoulder-down' variety, taking ½ g or more. The lighter the float, the more bites you will hit, as long as the float is heavy enough for the depth and conditions. For example, while ½ g is fine for this day's condition of no wind and in depths up to 8 ft, a bigger float will be preferable if it's windy in this depth, and in deeper water even if it's not windy. Carry ready-made 'eel rigs' with floats up to 2 g, although you should rarely have to use these bigger ones.

Leave your high-tech pole lines at home as well. Good, old-fashioned, abrasion-resistant reel lines are what's required, with 2 lb breaking strain for the main pole line and 1 lb or 1½ lb hooklengths. Hooks should also be chosen carefully, and many anglers prefer barbless patterns for eels

102

because they are easier to remove from an eel's mouth. Size 20 or 22 are best. Keep your shotting simple with an olivette and two or three small No. 8s underneath it. The distance of the weights from your hook is something that you will have to experiment with as eel bites are notoriously difficult to hit. Sometimes, you will hit most bites with the olivette 3 ft from the hook in 12 ft of water and the No. 8s equally spaced between this and the hook. On other occasions, your rig will work best with the olivette only 18 in from the hook and just a No. 8 between it and the hook. The answer, of course, is to experiment.

You should also try different depths. Start by plumbing carefully and trying to find any spot where a steep or gradual slope on the bottom flattens out. This area will be loved by eels, and you should start just at the point where it flattens out with your hookbait 1 in off the bottom. If you can get the eels to take the bait with your rig set like this, you will lip-hook most of them and will wonder what all the fuss was about. However, the times when you catch them like this are becoming increasingly rare. More often than not, you will need to fish with several inches of line on the bottom for the eels to take the hookbait with confidence. On other occasions, the eels will come right up off the bottom to intercept your loose feed as it falls through the water. This can be a recipe for disaster as most of the bites you get will be impossible to hit.

The way that you feed can help. Some top eel anglers swear by an approach best described as 'a lot and seldom', introducing perhaps 100 maggots at a time, and only adding more when they stop catching, or when bites become more difficult to hit. Others use the tried and tested 'little and often' feeding approach. This can also work. So can casters, especially if big eels are known to inhabit the venue you are fishing. In this case start by laying down a 'carpet' of a couple of good pouchfuls of casters, and then feed maggots. Try single and double maggot on the hook – sometimes the eels prefer one, sometimes two.

A word about those bites. You will miss a lot, but make things easy for yourself by using a float that has a thick, fluorescent tip. Quite often, an eel will take your maggot into its mouth sideways, moving on slowly to take a few others that you have loose fed before swallowing the lot. Strike with the maggot sideways in the eel's jaws and you will miss it, or hook it briefly before pulling out. You will see that your bait has been torn, curse under your breath, and rebait. The answer is to resist the urge to strike until the float has disappeared completely from view under the surface. When eels are feeding like this, it is normally shown in the float sinking slowly beneath the surface, staying there for several seconds before drifting out of sight completely. Resist the urge to strike until this second movement, hence the need for a tip that you can see easily. Agitate the bait frequently by lifting and lowering your pole. Eels are predators and they will rarely ignore a food item that is about to drift away.

One final tip. It is difficult to remove hooks out of eels. Make sure that you have plenty of hooks tied on from 6 in hooklengths and that they are easily accessible because you will undoubtedly lose a lot if you are catching a lot of eels. Once you have swung in your eel or netted it from the water, grasp it in either the landing net if you have netted it, the mouth of your keepnet, an old piece of netting material, a towel, or even by dropping it into a bucket of groundbait, sand or maizemeal. If you can see the maggot and hook, you should then be able to grasp and unhook the eel fairly easily before dropping it into your keepnet. If you cannot, try one attempt with a disgorger. If the hook does not come out, cut the line and tie on a new one.

Unhooking eels can be a tricky business.

CHAPTER NINE

CANALS

· ·

Cross over any canal bridge on a Saturday or Sunday and the chances are that you will see lines of anglers fishing a competition. Match fishing on canals is big business, from inner-city pub outings to grand open events. An increasing number of National Championships are being held on canals, and many World Championships as well. So what is it that canals offer as match venues? First, they are very fair. Most

Small fish like roach make up many canal match catches.

canals vary little along a match stretch, and the winning weight can be taken from many different pegs. Even if certain pegs stand out, good canal anglers can often make the prize list from anywhere. They also produce sport in most conditions from heatwave to snow and ice. When the rivers are in flood, thousands flock to canals, which are not affected so much by heavy rain. Of course they freeze over, but that doesn't stop match anglers and all sorts of ingenious devices have been invented to break the ice on a frozen canal.

Canals respond to all baits and all types of match angler, from the one who wants to catch large numbers of small fish to the one who is prepared to sit it out for a big carp. Urban canals and city canals can be equally productive and enjoyable places to fish. There's something strangely satisfying about catching fish among the factories, just as enjoyable as catching them out in the country. So let's take a look at the methods that the matchman will have to master if he is to become 'king of the cut'. Much of what follows applies to small waters such as drains as well as canals.

Match one

Venue - typical canal with a bloodworm ban.
Time of year - autumn.
Target species - small roach.

Hundreds of canal matches are held on venues just like this every weekend. They're usually extremely fair and the angler who wins with a catch of small roach can hold his head up high. Other species will figure as well, such as small perch, skimmer bream and gudgeon, but it is roach that will make up the bulk of anglers' catches. Typical canal roach average 20–40 to the pound so you will be talking about a lot of fish for a 5 lb catch, and even that might not be enough. For this example, however, we shall limit ourselves to catching small fish without worrying about larger ones at all.

What tackle do you need? The most important item is a pole. Ideally, you will need one that reaches across almost to the far bank. On most canals this will be from 11 m to 14 m, but don't worry if you do not have a pole of this length as there are ways round the problem. A rig of the same length as the top three sections of the pole will be required, or two rigs if possible with different-sized floats. On canals that are affected by surface tow caused by wind or the operation of the lock, use a float with a 'shoulder-up' body that will allow you to hold it back without it riding too far out from the surface. On still canals or those in which the water hardly moves, a 'shoulder-down' variety is best, with a wire stem and

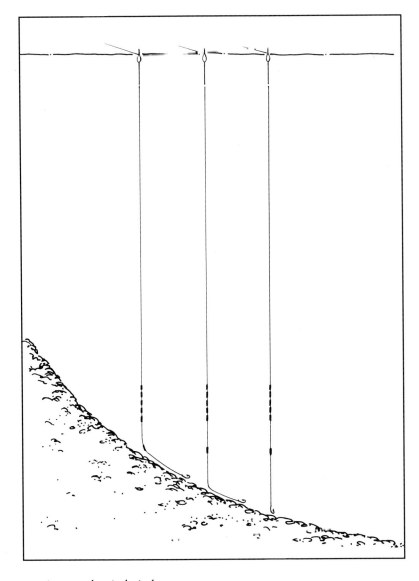

By adding or taking off a pole section, you fish at the bottom of the shelf, or up it.

a wire or plastic bristle.

One of these rigs should carry a float taking around five No. 12 styl weights and this can be shotted with small shot, cylindrical styls, or a small olivette plus one or two small weights underneath. Many canal roach anglers like to use several No 10. styls fixed close together around two-thirds of the way down between float and hook, with a No. 9, No. 8 and No. 7 styl underneath. This arrangement pulls the bait down fairly quickly to the lower layers of the canal where the fish will be lying early on in the match. However, once the match progresses and plenty of bait has been introduced, roach tend to move up in the water and a slowly falling bait might be required. Then it is just a case of separating the bunch of No 10. styls until they are equally spaced between

107

Right: Plumb the depth from above for the best reading.

Opposite: Draw the right peg and some big fish can be caught.

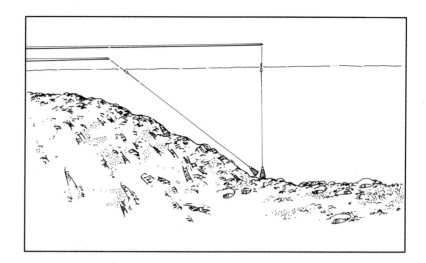

float and hook.

Your second pole rig should contain a lighter float taking, say, four No. 10 styls. This rig is for later on in the match, when the fish often 'creep' up on to the far shelf. By using a light float in the shallow water here, you should continue to catch them. Line length between pole tip and float is important. On still days or days when there is not much wind blowing, around 3 ft is ideal. However, on windy days, when the pole tip is being blown around, a longer line between float and pole tip will allow you to control the pole's movement without pulling the tackle around too much. For this sort of fishing, use a main line of around 0.09 mm diameter and a hooklength of 0.06 mm. Hooks should be of the fine-wire variety and no larger than a size 22.

As for bait, these small roach are suckers for squatts, but pinkies – especially fluorescent ones – can be useful, and you could take some hempseed as well. Groundbait is also necessary, and you should be looking for something fine so that it will disperse into an attractive cloud.

Plumb the depth carefully and try to discover where the bottom of the far shelf lies if you're fishing a canal. On a wider drain of similar depth, find a flat bit on the bottom that is far enough away from the near bank to allow you to establish a nearside swim as well without one interfering with the other. This spot at the bottom of the far shelf will be your main catching area, although as mentioned earlier the fish are likely to move up the shelf later in the match. Plumb the depth by starting with the pole at its full length and remove one section at a time, lowering your pole each time to check the depth. Reset your float and start again. When you are happy that the float is set correctly, mark your pole with a dab of white typewriter correcting fluid to tell you the depth. Then plumb much closer to the bank to discover the depth at

108

the bottom of the near shelf and mark this one as well. If it's not too windy, this nearside swim can be fished to-hand with a whip, but canal fish are becoming increasingly wary and the better presentation offered by a short line and longer pole is now usually more productive, if a little slower in the initial stages. As well as your pole, it is also worth setting up a small, all-balsa waggler taking, say, two BBs. Set this float to the same depth as your deeper pole rig for the far side and shot it just one or two small weights between float and hook. This waggler tackle can work well on prolific fisheries, but it has lost the edge that it had only a few years ago.

When the match starts, you should feed a couple of fist-sized balls of groundbait and three big catapult pouchfuls of hemp at the bottom of the far shelf. You should feed no squatts at this stage. Now begin fishing close in with your short line, adding a couple of sections to the pole, or with a whip and small olivette rig. Feed regularly with small pinches of groundbait, a few squatts and a smattering of hemp, and catch what you can here before moving across. The longer you manage to keep catching on the inside, the more confident the fish will be when you eventually move across, but you should not move across so late that you don't realise the full potential of this swim. Some 10 minutes before changing methods, start loose-feeding squatts over your initial consignment of hempseed and groundbait.

When you finally change depths and move out, the fish will hopefully be queuing up to be caught and you will continue catching on the far swim, finally moving right across with the lighter rig in the later stages. Feed loose-fed squatts. Only add more hemp and groundbait if a boat passes.

As you can see, such matches are quite clinical affairs but there are several places where skill and experience will take you one step ahead of your rivals. Plumb the depth carefully, move swims at the right time and feed the right amount for the amount of fish that are in your swim. In short, respond to what's happening in front of you and you're well on your way to a winning catch.

Match two

Venue - canal with far-bank features.
Time of year - summer.
Target species - big fish: carp, chub, roach, bream and perch.

Draw a peg on a canal with far-side features such as overhanging trees, bushes, or reeds and you would be foolish not to try to catch some of the big fish that are undoubtedly lurking there, the best bait for this being casters. Of course,

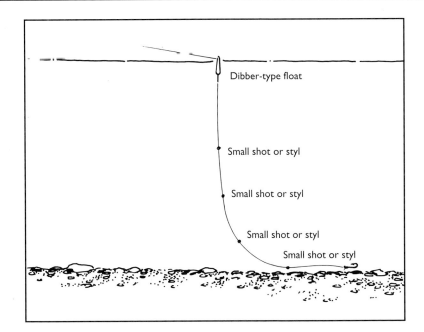

Dibber-type float

Small shot or styl

Small shot or styl

Small shot or styl

Small shot or styl

you can still fish the near and far sides as described above, although you would be wise to leave out the lightest float for fish with squatts and pinkies right across. Instead, use a pole-top kit with slightly stronger elastic such as No. 4 through the top two sections, and use a float designed for caster fishing. Because your bait will be fished well on the bottom, you need something a little more buoyant than a bristle, which would be pulled under by any surface tow. A float with a balsa top and wire stem is ideal, the top rounded off to combine buoyancy with sensitivity. Use a hooklength of 0.09 mm line and a size 18 caster hook to bury inside the bait. Plumb the depth carefully and set the float so that the bait is 6 in on the bottom. It's also worth setting up a slim quivertip rod with tackle that is relatively heavy for a canal - 1½ lb hooklength and size 16 or 18 strong hook.

Now fish the match exactly as described above, but every 10 minutes, carefully catapult half a dozen casters out close to the feature. If you see any signs of big fish bubbling or brushing the surface from underneath, try a single caster on the hook straight away with your caster rig on pole tackle. If you see nothing, it's worth trying this swim for 10 minutes every hour. Hook a good fish and the fun starts. If it's one of the hundreds of carp that live in most canals, you will have to be extremely skilful and fairly lucky to land it. If the carp moves away from the far side quickly, your chances are considerably increased. Just try to keep the pole above it, adding and taking off sections as required until it is ready for the net. Other species such as chub will also make for underwater snags with lightning speed, but big bream and

111

A good catch of canal bream for match-man Mark Bird.

roach are easier to subdue.

Of course, your light leger rod will subdue them quicker, especially if it's rigged with beefy tackle. Cast as close to the feature as you dare, and just wait for the rod to be pulled in! Fishing like this doesn't always work and it can be a difficult thing to do if anglers are catching small fish all around you, but all you need is one bite. Ring the changes with baits. Single and double caster, red maggots and double pinkie have all accounted for hundreds of good-quality canal fish, not only really big ones, but bigger-than-average roach as well. You can soon stride ahead, catching 3 oz roach when everyone else is catching ½ oz ones.

CHOPPED WORM

Match three

Venue - clear canal or drain.
Time of year - winter.
Target species - perch.

Here is a match that is tailor-made for a method fairly new to British match fishing. Chopped worms as feed combined with a small piece of worm on the hook has been found to be a devastating way of catching on hard-fished canals. It tempts perch and ruffe predominantly, but other species as well and is at its best in winter and when the water is clear. However, chopped worm will work at any time of the year if there is colour in the water. Perch in particular, being predators, are attracted by small pieces introduced into the swim, playing around with the chopped up worms and working themselves into a feeding frenzy. Once a redworm hookbait is presented in front of them, they will take it almost without hesitation. It should be fished on pole tackle, and down the shelf towards the deepest water in the centre. The chopped-lobworm feed is introduced in a small cup clipped on to the pole near its tip, and the hookbait is fished under a light float taking only three or four No. 12 styls, shotted simply with a small bulk and two small weights underneath. The hook should be small but strong, and have a wide gape. Plumb the depth carefully and fish with the hookbait 1 in off the bottom.

Start the match by feeding three lobworms. These are now available from many tackle shops, although it's much cheaper and great fun to collect them yourself on a lawn during warm, damp nights. Drop the lobworms into the cup and chop them up with a pair of small, sharp scissors. Then carefully ship the pole out to your chosen fishing spot and drop the worms into

Use scissors to chop your worms.

A rig for chopped worm fishing.

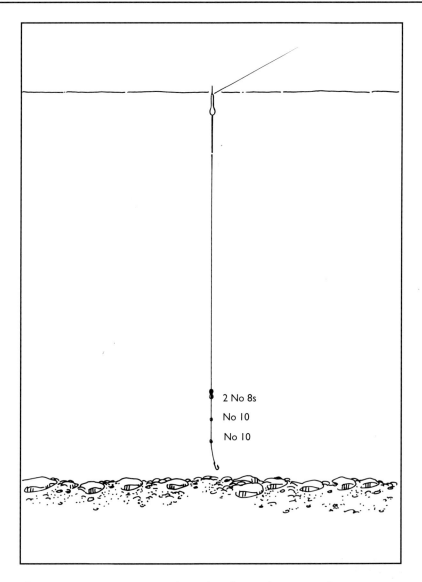

2 No 8s

No 10

No 10

the swim. You may need to dip the pole tip in the water to dampen the inside of the cup in order to release the worms. Now retrieve the pole, unclip the cup, and hook a small redworm, cutting it so a small amount of juices are being released from one end. All you have to do now is ship the pole out again and drop the tackle over the feed. If there are perch near by, you should get bites straight away and the action will begin. Add more chopped lobworms if bites start to tail off, or if you are catching so well that you suspect all the food might soon be eaten. Agitate the tackle constantly, as perch in particular will take a bait that is moving. When other baits are not working, chopped worm can be a winner, but it's unlikely to beat more conventional tactics unless big perch are present.

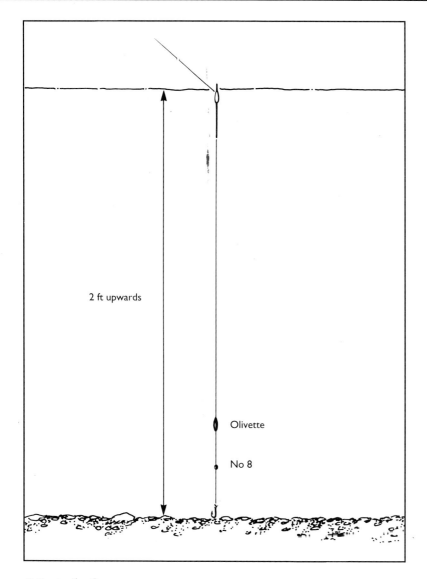

2 ft upwards

Olivette

No 8

Match four

Venue - hard-fished canal.
Time of year - autumn.
Target species - small fish, roach, perch and gudgeon.

This type of canal match is best tackled with bloodworm and jokers, as long as they are not banned. If they are allowed, you can be certain that they are the most widely used baits on the canal, especially in matches where it is unlikely that any other bait will come close for fish-catching potential. Although obtaining these two baits can be difficult and expensive, fishing with them is relatively easy. In truth, there is usually a bait dealer in attendance at matches where

115

Right: Bloodworms and jokers are good where they are allowed.

Opposite: Using a pole cup takes a little practise.

bloodworm and jokers are allowed, and he will be able to supply your bait, as long as you order it in advance. For a typical contest where small fish are the quarry, you will need 1 pt of jokers and enough bloodworms for use as hookbait. Special bloodworm 'hooker packs' are available. Both will be supplied carefully folded in newspaper and ideally in their 'raw' state, with nothing else in among them. You might pick up your bait to find that it has been mixed with damp peat, or even dried and broken up leaves. Such bait is probably a few days old, so check it carefully and if you're not happy with it, tell the supplier. Most are reliable and will provide good bait when you want it.

Bloodworms are used mainly as hookbait over joker feed, and there are several different ways of introducing jokers to your swim. Only you can decide which approach to adopt, but if in doubt, err on the cautious. The extreme method is the Continental-style bait bombardment that is such a feature of World Championship matches. Here most of the jokers are mixed up with groundbait and several big balls are thrown into the swim at the start of the match. This rarely works in this country, and you would be far better off adopting a much more delicate approach to your swim. Groundbait can still be used, but in much smaller amounts and even that might be too much. In you are in any doubt, leave the groundbait out altogether and feed your jokers raw, or with a little damp clay or leam added to make them stick together, and instead of throwing them into the swim, use a pole cup.

That apart, the approach and rigs are similar to those required in a match where squatt is the main bait. However, you can try floats with wire bristles. These floats, although difficult to shot correctly – so that just a small part of the bristle is showing at the surface – are extremely sensitive and in keeping with delicate baits such as bloodworm and joker. Have a jar of grease handy to dip the float tip into at regular intervals throughout the match if it sinks a little too much to be able to be seen clearly. Special coloured grease is now available and a float, when treated, becomes the ultimate sensitive indicator of a bite.

Plumb the depth carefully and try to concentrate your feed at the bottom of both shelves and along the middle if there is no boat traffic. At the start, introduce two cupfuls on the far line, depositing the bait carefully into the right spot. Cupping any bait takes a bit of practice, especially if you are fishing from a narrow canal towpath and are using 11 m or more of pole. High banks behind can make life difficult on drains as well. Practice makes perfect, and it's worth spending time in the back garden, using soil instead of bait. The problem is that the bait often jumps out as the pole is being pushed out. There is no secret formula, but as you become more experienced in the art of cupping, you will become faster, and soon you'll wonder what all the fuss was about.

Feed the closer swim on the little-and-often principle, either with a small cup the same size as a thimble, or by throwing in small balls of jokers mixed with damp clay no larger than your thumbnail. Start on this close-in line, but as soon as bites start to slow down, move across to another fed area, take a few fish, move to another a little later, then try close in again, until eventually you start to catch more quickly in one area. By this time, the match should be at least three hours old and you can spend the last couple of hours really going to town on the most prolific swim. This will usually be the one at the bottom of the far shelf, and you should top this one up with more cups of joker if bites here start to slow. If bites continue thick and fast, there is obviously enough bait to keep the fish happy so there's no point in introducing more.

You can store your bloodworm hookbait either in a little water – after all, they came from water in the first place – or in its bought state in a lidded box. Select good-sized bloodworms for the hook initially, and use a fine-wire size 24, but be prepared to experiment with smaller bloodworms or even single and double joker on the hook if bites are hard to come by. Whether you use bloodworm or joker on the hook, hook the bait very carefully in the second segment from the rounded end.

Of course, you can add other canal methods to your bloodworm and joker approach. If you're opposite a bush, for example, a few casters fired across at regular intervals by catapult will do no harm. Introduce a few in with your jokers on your intended main catching area to help hold any larger fish should they appear in the swim. This approach and light rigs will work for roach and perch, but if you plan an all-out assault on a canal's gudgeon population, use bigger floats taking up to $1\frac{1}{2}$ g with an olivette and one or two dropper shot underneath that will take the bait quickly down to the bottom. It is also a good idea to use a cane-stemmed float that will accentuate bites if fish take the bait before the dropper shot have settled. Gudgeon will do this frequently if there are many of them in the swim and they are competing for food. Small, hard balls of jokers in groundbait (summer) or leam (winter) are required here. Again, you might find that a close-in gudgeon swim starts to tail off some time into the match. By moving out to one of your other baited swims, you will probably be able to return to this swim later and continue catching fish. Exhaust it early and that's your lot for the whole match.

If you manage to keep a bloodworm and joker swim active for the whole match so that you are still catching at the end, you should be very pleased with yourself and feel satisfied that you have fed and fished correctly. The chances are that you will finish in the prize list as well, especially if you have managed to catch a few bonus fish on caster.

CHAPTER TEN

FISHING A NATIONAL

Get everything right and you could be celebrating like this.

National Championships remain at the pinnacle of most match anglers' careers. After graduating from pleasure angler to match angler, through club events to open competitions, the time comes when you're given the chance to fish in a National. With six divisions of 90 teams and 12 anglers in a team, more than 6,000 anglers fish Nationals every season. No longer are they the elitist 'All-England' events, and while many top match anglers would bemoan the loss of one big National, they are forgetting about the thousands of anglers who, if that remained the case, would never get the opportunity to compete in an event that offers a real chance of glory and big cash prizes. In truth, there's much more to fishing a National than winning. Taking part is something in itself, for the atmosphere at all Nationals, Division One or Division Six, is very special. Even if you are not an open match angler, the expansion of the divisions has allowed clubs to take part as long as they pay an affiliation fee to the

Fishing your first national can be a daunting experience.

organisers – the National Federation of Anglers. Then, if that club of perhaps only 20 members put in the work required in practice, there's no reason why they shouldn't be called up to the rostrum to receive their winners' medals. There are few greater feelings in angling than to be recognised by your fellow anglers.

Nationals are run like any other team match that is decided on points. One member of each 12-angler team fishes in each section. The sections are given letters A to M (omitting I because of the confusion with the figure 1), and each angler is allocated a section by computer at NFA headquarters in Derby. This section draw is kept secret and nobody knows

The crowds gather as Jeff Perrin fishes the John Smith's Championships.

until the morning of the match in what section he is to fish. When the team captains line up to make the draw, they tell the organisers the name of their team. The captains are then given a sealed envelope containing the predetermined section draw (team members' names and pools money have to be supplied months in advance, although team changes can be made on the day). Then they draw a peg number, just as in any other match. Each of the team then fishes that peg number in their section.

Then the fun really starts. Instead of over 1,000 anglers making their way to their allotted sections, coaches are laid on for the purpose. Each angler has to find the coach marked with his section – C1-24, for example – load his gear on, and travel to the section. National novices find these trips awe-inspiring. Everyone seems to know everything about their section except you, so all you do is sit quietly saying nothing. Don't worry. They are probably as much in the dark as you are and simply putting on a brave face. Those who really know the score are likely to be sitting as quietly as you, smiling silently to themselves about the comments that are being made. Once the coach arrives at the water, there's something of a free-for-all when all the fishing tackle is unloaded, after which you have to find your way to your peg. Stewards – each team has to provide two – will probably check your tackle for signs of banned bait, and at this point it is worth having a quick chat with them to make friends. Getting the stewards on your side can work to your advantage when it comes to keeping anglers back from the skyline or even finding out what's happening elsewhere in your section. After that, it's just like any other match fished to NFA rules.

When the whistle goes for the end of the contest, do not leave your peg until you have been weighed in. Stewards will do this, but check the scales and check also that your weight has been correctly recorded on the weigh-in cards. Nationals have been won and lost through stewards' errors, although thankfully these are now very rare occurrences. The weigh-in completed, every angler makes his way back to the coach, the register is called, the coach returns to the headquarters and you can relay your tales of success or woe to your team-mates.

It takes only a couple of hours for the results to be announced, during which time the tension can be tremendous, especially if your team is in with a chance of promotion. Each National has 15 teams that are promoted (except Division One) and 15 that are relegated (except the bottom division, unless a new division is to be created because more teams have joined the NFA). Results are worked out on a points basis, with each section winner receiving the same number of points as there are teams competing in the match. With a bookie in attendance, cash is handed out to the victors, although pools winnings are sent later in cheque form from the organisers.

Preparation for a National

So much for the running of a National, but what about the preparation? When should that begin? Of course, that all depends on how seriously you intend to take the match. For many teams, it is the highlight of the season and they spend months getting ready for this one match. For them, any result apart from promotion is a disaster. Other teams treat Nationals as days out, and enjoy every minute without even thinking about the match beforehand. Practice sessions are avoided and preparations kept to a minimum. For these teams, it is a bonus not to be relegated.

However, if you want to do well, there is no substitute for hard work, and by doing just this several teams have risen to the top division in only a few years, no mean feat when most of the annual matches have taken place on different venues. For a team to do well, you need 12 good anglers who have nothing less than total commitment. That is something few teams can boast and you can still be reasonably successful without this commitment until you reach the very top and compete against teams whose captains and sponsors expect nothing less than total professionalism. But what about most teams preparing for a National? Even if the commitment is there, few teams, especially those in the lower divisions, will have 12 very good anglers. They might have eight, or even 10, but in a points match like a National Championships, no team looking to mount a serious challenge can afford to 'carry' anyone. This is where practice comes in, because even a mediocre team can still perform well in a National Championship by putting in the time and effort required to succeed.

Preparations should begin as soon as you know where you will be fishing, usually one year in advance of the match itself. These preparations can take many forms. Any team that really means business should visit the venue at least once during the season before their National. This way they can start to familiarise themselves with the place. The fishing might be very different from what it will be on National day, but don't worry about that. Getting to grips with the venue is what it's all about, learning its moods, fishing it in different conditions and pooling all this valuable information together. Once you're into the new season, serious practice should begin. Clubs on whose fisheries Nationals are held will almost

123

Help from local experts can be invaluable in your preparations.

certainly be running several open events leading up to the big day. Attend as many as you can, either to fish or simply to watch. Really there's no substitute for fishing, but make sure that you follow the weigh-in to assess your performance relative to others in your section. If anyone has beaten you, try to find out how they fished. Regular team meetings are important, and the captain should start to compile a dossier on his team members' performances, not only to gather information about the venue, but also to help with team selection.

It is extremely useful when preparing for a National to acquire some local help. Get in quickly and you can probably obtain the services of a good angler who will be able to pass on hints and tips about the venue and its methods. Listen carefully to what he has to say and adapt his comments to your own findings. Don't make the mistake of taking absolutely everything that he says as gospel, remembering that many local experts fish every match to win as an individual, which could be fatal for a team wanting to do well. A closed-season outing with your local expert can give you a good grounding, especially if he takes you to several different spots along the match length. It would also be a good idea if he took some tackle along with him to demonstrate some of the rigs and methods required, perhaps even plumbing the depth at each spot. Be generous with your tutor and he will look after you as well. Some sort of payment certainly wouldn't go amiss. Try also to ensure that he spends National day with the team, as last-minute advice on the conditions on the day might be important.

Left: Even twice world champion Bob Nudd has to prepare.

Below: Work hard in match fishing and you could be like Dave Wesson, 1992 world champion at the age of 21!

Some venues lend themselves to team tactics, others don't, and it's a foolish team captain who tells his team that all must fish in a certain way just like robots. If the team has prepared well enough, the captain won't have to say anything to his team. They should all know what is required and what they have to do. It is far better for a team to learn among themselves and agree a method if one has emerged as the best. This might be the case on a canal, but it's hardly likely on a natural river where different areas of the match length will respond to different methods. On natural venues such as this, the strongest teams in terms of skill and experience will show their true worth, but on canals where much of the match length will be similar, teams who have practised and shown all-round commitment can also put on a good performance.

To give you an idea of the preparation involved in a

125

National, here's a year in the life of a squad intending to do well in the Championships. Let's assume that the match takes place in July.

August (the previous year) – find out the venue and acquire the services of a local expert.

September – visit the venue, preferably for a team competition. Most of the squad should fish, but a few can walk the bank, watching for likely methods and techniques that might work on the big day. However, don't take too much notice of the result as a venue in September can fish differently to one in July.

October to April – contact should be maintained between team captain or manager and the local expert enlisted to help.

March – book tickets for matches leading up to the event. Book time off work for anyone who is able to spend a week practising on the venue. This should be the last available practice week. National venues are closed to competitors for six days before the match.

April – the whole squad should visit the venue some time in the closed season with the local expert. Walk as many sections as you can, with the expert demonstrating techniques and rigs, offering advice and pinpointing good areas. As it is the closed season, he cannot fish, but he can still give you a detailed insight into the venue. If possible, make a video of the day. This is also the time to pay entry fees and pools to the National Federation of Anglers, and a good time to sort out the two stewards that you will need.

May – produce a transcript of the video and discuss this and the day spent with the expert at a team meeting.

June – practice proper begins with the start of the season. With the match in July, there are only a few weeks, so practice will have to be intense. Every member of the squad should fish several matches, and also walk the bank to see what others are doing. Assess every performance and try to see whether a pattern emerges. Those who are spending the week practising should try different and unusual methods to provide contingency plans should the main approach go wrong. Make numerous telephone calls during the week to check everything is going to plan. If any of the squad feel that they are not confident on the venue by now, they should be honest enough to admit it.

July – the week before the match sees the last and all-important squad meeting where final methods are discussed and agreed. Confidence should be high for any squad that has worked this hard, and anyone who doesn't make the final 12 is bound to be disappointed. However, team fishing isn't just about those anglers fishing the match, and everybody in the squad should feel a part of what, hopefully, will be a successful National Championships on the day.

INDEX

Other Fishing Titles Available from Boxtree:

1-85283-181-2	Wilson's Angle	£9.99
1-85283-182-0	Go Fishing Year	£10.99
1-85283-156-1	Go Fishing	£9.99

Improve Your Coarse Fishing Series:

1-85283-190-1	Float Fishing	£9.99
1-85283-187-1	Pole Fishing	£9.99
1-85283-188-X	Legering	£12.99
1-85283-189-8	Baits	£12.99
1-85283-444-7	Specimen Hunting	£12.99

Angling Times Library:

1-85283-122-7	1: Carp	£9.99
1-85283-123-5	2: Tench	£9.99
1-85283-124-3	3: Chub	£9.99
1-85283-126-X	4: Pike	£9.99
1-85283-152-9	5: Bream	£12.99
1-85283-153-7	6: Barbel	£12.99
1-85283-151-0	7: Roach, Rudd & Dace	£12.99

All these books are available at your local bookshop or newsagent, or can be ordered direct from Littlehampton Book Services, tel: 0903 726 410.

Prices and availability subject to change without notice.

YOU'VE READ THE BOOK NOW READ THE MAGAZINE!

Improve Your Coarse Fishing magazine is Britain's best selling fishing monthly and is always full of great articles, tackle reviews and hundreds of hints and tips from all the best anglers to help you catch more fish and enjoy your sport.

If you want to improve your angling technique then this is the magazine for you.

Improve Your Coarse Fishing is on sale from the 19th of every month.